Charismatic

Catechism

Charismatic Catechism

BY

ERNEST B. GENTILE

NEW LEAF PRESS
Box 1045 Harrison Ark 72601

Library of Congress Catalog Card Number: 76-22255

International Standard Book Number: 0-89221-025-7

Second Printing, December 1979

Cover illustration after painting by J. C. Leyendecker

DEDICATION

To my wife Joy, my children and
all the wonderful helpers that have
made being a pastor and a Christian
such a happy experience.

FOREWORD

In a world of confusion and darkness, Light is breaking forth. God, by His Spirit, is raising up a generation of believers who are seeking the spiritual balance needed to produce effective Christians in this hour. The tendency in Christendom has been to go to the extreme of either intellectualism or emotionalism — either all Word or all Spirit. We thank God that He is raising up His Church in these days to become well balanced followers of Jesus Christ.

Pastor Ernest Gentile's ministry in writing is being used of God to impart a depth of understanding of the Word of God and the moving of the Spirit of God in these last days.

For over four years we have been using Pastor Gentile's catechism book as a basic doctrine course in our high school department, and now it is being used as a regular course in the curriculum of our Bible College. I personally believe that this course is one of the reasons that our teen-agers have become stabilized in an unstable world. God requires Christians to be able to give the reason or the hope that is in them (1 Peter 3:15). The Amplified Version of Proverbs 18:13 says: "He who answers a matter before he hears the facts, it is folly and shame to him."

In examining the evidence of Christian religion it is essential for the discovery of Truth that our mind be free from all former prejudices, as well as be open to conviction. There must be readiness on our part to investigate with candor, then follow the Truth wherever it may lead us.

It is with appreciation that I have followed the concise approach Pastor Gentile uses in his clear teaching of Truth. I am sure that this book will be a strength and blessing to the reader, even as it has been to our people at Bible Temple.

Pastor K.R. Iverson

President of
Portland Bible College
Portland, Oregon

PREFACE

This book uses an ancient, simple technique in teaching Bible truths. It is called a "catechism" because it employs the question-and-answer method. For each subject I have chosen what I feel to be the vital, most-asked questions on that subject; then, I have attempted to give concise, practical answers based on Bible truths.

The catechetical method of instruction is one of proved value. The word "catechism" need not imply dry, uninteresting religious instruction. We have taught the following material as a catechism course in our church for the past fourteen years, and it has proven to be a great blessing to our people. Other churches have also used this basic material in a profitable way. Each time the course has been taught, I have attempted to streamline the lessons and make it as practical as possible. This book is designed so that it can be used profitably as a one-year course of Bible indoctrination for beginning Bible students.

In preparing this book I have carefully examined and compared the material presented in five other catechisms: two of Martin Luther's Catechisms, the Roman Catholic Catechism, "Understanding God" by Patricia Gruits, and the "Church School Bible Course" by Maureen Gaglardi. Each of these works has made its own significant contribution to Bible teaching, and I hope that my particular approach will also prove to be helpful. I am grateful for the permission extended to me to draw on some of the information in the works of Gruits and Gaglardi. I am also indebted to the late Pastor W. H. Offiler for his concept of "God's Plan of the Ages."

Please take time to examine the Table of Contents; each lesson has a special significance when viewed against the over-all approach. Note that you have before you a study of basic Old Testament truths contrasted with New Testament teaching. Also, you will discover that the lessons unfold God's own nature as Father, Son, and Holy Spirit. The closing chapters on the Church are but the opening thoughts on the exciting adventure of living the life meant for New Testament Christians. May the Lord bless this study to you in a rich way!

1976   Ernest B. Gentile

CONTENTS

CONTENTS

PART I.
THE IMPORTANCE OF YOUR BIBLE

PART I. THE IMPORTANCE OF YOUR BIBLE

PART I. THE IMPORTANCE OF YOUR BIBLE

LESSON 1: BASIC QUESTIONS ABOUT THE BIBLE

✓1. WHAT IS THE BIBLE?

    The Bible is the written Word of God. John 17:17; 20:31.

✓2. WHO PRODUCED THE BIBLE?

    God is the author of the Bible, and holy men of God were used to actually express His thoughts in writing. Prophets and priests wrote the Old Testament, and the evangelists and apostles wrote the books of the New Testament. 2 Peter 1:21; Revelation 22:18.

3. WHAT DOES "THE WORD OF GOD" MEAN?

    "The Word of God" means that God has spoken or expressed Himself. Just as we exchange ideas by speaking words, God talks to us by using words (or, THE Word). John 1:1; 1 Peter 1:23, 25; Hebrews 1:1.

4. WHY IS THE BIBLE THE WORD OF GOD ALTHOUGH IT WAS WRITTEN BY MAN?

    The Bible is the Word of God because these writers were inspired of God to write His thoughts. 2 Timothy 3:16; 1 Thessalonians 2:13.

5. WHAT DOES "BY INSPIRATION OF GOD" MEAN?

    "By inspiration of God" means that God breathed His thoughts into the minds of men, so that these men expressed exactly the very thoughts of God. 2 Peter 1:21; 1 Corinthians 2:13.

6. WHAT DO WE MEAN WHEN WE SAY THAT THE ENTIRE BIBLE IS INSPIRED?

    Every word of the Bible is God's Word; therefore, there are no errors or mistakes in the Bible. The power of inspiration kept the writers from making any mistakes. John 10:35; 17:17; 2 Timothy 3:16.

7. FOR WHAT PURPOSE DID GOD GIVE US THE BIBLE?

    God gave us the Bible so that we can understand His will and purpose about things that are spiritual or earthly. 2 Timothy 3:15-17; Psalm 119:105.

8. WHAT USE SHOULD WE MAKE OF THE BIBLE?

    We should diligently and reverently read and study the Bible, listen attentively when it is read and explained, believe it, and live according to it. John 5:39; 14:23; Luke 11:28.

9. HOW CAN WE KNOW THE TRUE MEANING OF THE BIBLE? 1 Corinthians 2:14.

    Four things are essential to understand the Bible: [1] You must be a child of God. [2] You must be inspired by God's Spirit. [3] You must read and study with an open mind (free from prejudice). [4] You must receive teaching and instruction from God-inspired ministries set in the Church.

10. **WHAT ARE THE TWO GREAT DOCTRINES OF THE BIBLE?**
Law and Gospel are the two great doctrines of the Bible.

11. **WHAT IS THE LAW?**
The Law is that doctrine of the Bible in which God tells us how we are to be and what we are to do and not to do. Leviticus 19:2; Exodus 24:11; and Deuteronomy 6:6, 7.

12. **WHAT IS THE GOSPEL?**
"Gospel" means "Good News." The Gospel is that doctrine of the Bible in which God tells us the good news of our salvation in Jesus Christ. 1 John 4:9; John 3:16; Romans 1:16.

13. **WHAT IS THE DIFFERENCE BETWEEN THE LAW AND THE GOSPEL?**
A. The Law teaches what we are to do and not to do; and the Gospel teaches what God has done, and still does, for our Salvation.
B. The Law shows us our sin and the wrath of God; the Gospel shows us our Saviour and the Grace of God.

LESSON 1 STUDY QUESTIONS BASED ON "BASIC QUESTIONS ABOUT THE BIBLE"

1. What is the Bible?
2. Who produced the Bible?
3. What does "The Word of God" mean?
4. Why is the Bible the Word of God although it was written by man?
5. What does "By Inspiration of God" mean?
6. What do we mean when we say that the entire Bible is inspired?
7. For what purpose did God give us the Bible?
8. What use should we make of the Bible?
9. How can we know the true meaning of the Bible?
10. What are the two great doctrines of the Bible?
11. What is the Law?
12. What is the Gospel?
13. What is the difference between the Law and the Gospel?
14. Memorize Psalms 119:105; John 3:16 and Romans 1:16.

LESSON 2: THE BIBLE IS A DIVINE LIBRARY

1.   WHAT ARE THE BOOKS OF THE BIBLE?
   The Bible is not simply one book, but rather a library or compilation of sixty-six books bound together. Every Christian should know the books of the Holy Bible so that he can easily find the Scripture he is desirous of reading. They are easily memorized if taken in groups as listed below. Since both the Old Testament and the New Testament have FIVE MAJOR sections each, an easy memory aid to help remember the sections is the use of the FIVE FINGERS on each hand.

OLD TESTAMENT

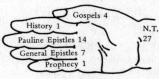

THE LAW [5]
GENESIS
EXODUS
LEVITICUS
NUMBERS
DEUTERONOMY

HISTORY [12]
JOSHUA
JUDGES
RUTH
1 SAMUEL
2 SAMUEL
1 KINGS
2 KINGS
1 CHRONICLES
2 CHRONICLES
EZRA
NEHEMIAH
ESTHER

POETRY [5]
JOB
PSALMS
PROVERBS
ECCLESIASTES
SONG OF SOLOMON

MAJOR PROPHETS [5]
ISAIAH
JEREMIAH
LAMENTATIONS
EZEKIEL
DANIEL

MINOR PROPHETS [12]
HOSEA
JOEL
AMOS
OBADIAH
JONAH
MICAH
NAHUM
HABAKKUK
ZEPHANIAH
HAGGAI
ZECHARIAH
MALACHI

NEW TESTAMENT

THE GOSPELS [4]
MATTHEW
MARK
LUKE
JOHN

HISTORY [1]
THE ACTS

PAULINE EPISTLES [14]
ROMANS
1 CORINTHIANS
2 CORINTHIANS
GALATIANS
EPHESIANS
PHILIPPIANS
COLOSSIANS

1 THESSALONIANS
2 THESSALONIANS
1 TIMOTHY
2 TIMOTHY
TITUS
PHILEMON
HEBREWS

GENERAL EPISTLES [7]
JAMES
1 PETER
2 PETER
1 JOHN
2 JOHN
3 JOHN
JUDE

PROPHECY [1]
THE REVELATION

17

2. HOW IS THE BIBLE DIVIDED?

    The Bible is divided into the Old Testament, written before the coming of Jesus Christ, and the New Testament written after His ascension into Heaven. 2 Corinthians 3:14, 16.

3. HOW MANY MEN DID GOD USE IN WRITING THE BIBLE?

    Approximately 44 writers were used by God in the course of twenty centuries to write the Bible. Jeremiah 36:18; Galatians 6:11; 2 Thessalonians 3:17.

4. SOME INTERESTING FACTS ABOUT THE BIBLE:

    There are 1189 chapters in the Bible; 919 in the Old Testament; 260 in the New Testament.

    The longest chapter is Psalms 119. The shortest chapter is Psalms 117 which is also the middle chapter of the Bible.

    The longest verse is Esther 8:9. The shortest verse, John 11:35.

    The Old Testament is approximately 3-1/2 times the size of the New Testament.

5. AN EXPLANATION OF HOW SCRIPTURE REFERENCES ARE WRITTEN.

    Usually Scripture references are abbreviated. If a person is taking notes, he will find it quite helpful in conserving time and space to use the following traditional approach.

    FIRST, the book; SECOND, the chapter; THIRD, the verse or verses.

    "Rev. 3:20" means the Book of Revelation, chapter three, verse twenty. The colon is used to separate chapter and verse; commas are used to separate verses; thus Rev. 3:19, 20 would refer to verses nineteen and twenty. Dashes indicate the inclusion of all the verses between two numbers; as, Rev. 3:19-21 refers to verses nineteen through twenty-one. Semi-colons are used to separate different references.

LESSON 2 STUDY QUESTIONS BASED ON "THE BIBLE IS A DIVINE LIBRARY"

1. How is the Bible divided?
2. How many Books are in the Bible? How many are in the Old Testament? How many are in the New Testament?
3. Into what five sections is the Old Testament divided?
4. Into what five sections is the New Testament divided?
5. Write and be able to recite the Books of the Old Testament.
6. Write and be able to recite the Books of the New Testament.
7. How many men did God use in writing the Bible?
8. How much larger than the New Testament is the Old Testament?

LESSON 3: WHY WE SHOULD USE OUR BIBLE

1. HOW CAN I DECIDE TO BECOME A SERIOUS STUDENT OF THE BIBLE?
You will become a daily, serious student of the Bible when you realize that you absolutely need it. Many believe they SHOULD study the Bible, but few are convinced that such study is indispensable. Jeremiah 15:16; Ezekiel 2:8.

2. WHAT WILL THE STUDY OF THE BIBLE DO FOR ME?
Here are just seven things that Bible study will do for you:
[1] Bible Study UNCOVERS sin and mistakes.
  Hebrews 4:12; 2 Timothy 3:16; James 1:23, 24.
[2] Bible Study CLEANSES us from the pollutions of sin.
  1 John 1:9; Psalms 119:9; John 15:3; 17:17; Ephesians 5:25, 26.
[3] Bible Study IMPARTS STRENGTH.
  Deuteronomy 8:3; Matthew 4:4; Psalms 19:10; 119:103; Job 23:12; Jeremiah 15:16; Ezekiel 2:8-3:3; Revelation 10:9, 10. Scriptures are called "milk" — 1 Peter 2:2; 1 Corinthians 3:2; Hebrews 5:12, 13; Acts 20:32; 2 Timothy 4:1-4; 1 John 2:14.
[4] Bible Study INSTRUCTS us in what we are to do.
  Matthew 7:24-27; James 1:22.
[5] Bible Study PROVIDES US A SWORD for victory over sin.
  Ephesians 6:17; Psalms 119:11.
[6] Bible Study MAKES OUR LIVES FRUITFUL AND PROSPEROUS.
  Psalms 1:1-3; Joshua 1:8; 3 John 2.
[7] Bible Study gives us POWER TO PRAY.
  John 15:7; 2 Timothy 3:14-17.

3. THE BIBLE IS ITS OWN BEST COMMENTARY!
Every Bible student should have a good concordance and Bible dictionary, as well as various translations and versions to illuminate the meaning of the original text. IT IS A MISTAKE, however, to load yourself down with many books which INTERPRET the Bible; you will note that the false cult teachers always do this to their new converts. We contend that YOUR OWN BIBLE, through the use of cross references and subject index, is its own best interpreter and commentary.

LESSON 4: SOME THINGS YOU SHOULD KNOW ABOUT YOUR BIBLE

1. WHY ARE SOME WORDS IN THE KING JAMES VERSION IN ITALICS?
Italicized words in the King James Version were written this way by the translators to let us know that the words were not in the original Hebrew or Greek text; they merely help to express the meaning of the verse.

2. WHAT DOES THIS SIGN (¶) MEAN?
This is a paragraph sign, which means (usually) that the verses between two of these signs refer to the same theme or subject.

3. ARE THE CHAPTER NUMBERS AND VERSE NUMBERS INSPIRED BY GOD?
   No. These have been included in Bibles by the translators as an aid for quick reference. Generally they follow the basic thought breaks. Unfortunately, there are places where the chapter or verse notation interrupts the flow of thought; for instance, 1 Corinthians 12:31 and 13:1.

4. WHAT DO YOU DO WHEN YOU FIND A WORD IN THE BIBLE THAT YOU DON'T UNDERSTAND?
   The answer is simple — you look it up! Some words are explained in your regular dictionary, whereas other words will have more explanation in a Bible dictionary. Don't be discouraged, since there are only about 6,000 different English words in the entire Bible, you'll soon be moving easily through its pages.

5. WHY HAVE A "CENTER COLUMN REFERENCE"?
   Your study Bible probably will have a column down the middle of each page. This handy reference column is filled with other Bible references for the various verses as well as amplified word meanings for the more difficult words. This column will be of great help to you!

6. HOW SHOULD I USE MY CENTER COLUMN REFERENCE?
   When you see a small letter beside a Bible statement, look that letter up in the center column; the Bible references beside it will be concerned with the same subject. If there is a small numeral beside a word, you will find that numeral repeated in the center column with additional meaning for that word in italics (this meaning is based on the original language).

LESSONS 3 AND 4 STUDY QUESTIONS BASED ON
"WHY WE SHOULD USE OUR BIBLE" and
"SOME THINGS YOU SHOULD KNOW ABOUT YOUR BIBLE"

1. How can I decide to become a serious student of the Bible?
2. Name seven things that Bible study will do for you.
3. What is the Bible's best commentary?
4. Why are some words in the King James Version in italics?
5. What is the "paragraph sign" and what does it mean?
6. Are the chapter numbers and verse numbers inspired by God?
7. What do you do when you find a word in the Bible that you don't understand?
8. Why have a "center column reference"?
9. How should I use my Center Column Reference?

LESSON 5: HOW TO STUDY THE BIBLE

NOTE: To thoroughly know the Bible, it is ESSENTIAL that we be taught by the Holy Spirit through teaching ministries (Ephesians 4:11, 12). But it is equally important that you develop a personal experience with the Word of Life through a proper study pattern. Memorize 2 Timothy 2:15.

1. WHERE IS THE BEST PLACE TO BEGIN IN READING THE WHOLE BIBLE? Start reading in Matthew and continue through to Revelation. Then, begin in Genesis and read right through to Revelation. Read the Bible again from Genesis to Revelation, and continue re-reading the Bible like this ALL OF THE REST OF YOUR CHRISTIAN LIFE!

2. IS IT NECESSARY TO READ EVERY CHAPTER? Read the WHOLE Bible, chapter by chapter, reading every word and marking your Bible as you proceed.

3. HOW SHOULD I STUDY THE BIBLE — BY BOOKS, CHAPTERS OR VERSES? For daily devotional reading, the average Christian will find it best to study the Bible by chapters. Some books like Jonah or Jude can be read easily at a single sitting, but the Gospel of Matthew would take two hours of hard concentration. For daily benefit, we recommend that you study by chapters, rather than by TOO BIG or TOO SMALL Scripture portions.

4. DO THESE TWO THINGS WHEN STUDYING THE BIBLE BY CHAPTERS. After reading a chapter of the Bible, do not leave it until:
   [1] You have made a simple outline of that chapter.
   [2] You have found some great truth or development of some theme.

5. SHOULD I EXPECT TO GET SOMETHING OUT OF EVERY CHAPTER? It is important that no passage of the Bible remain a barren area to you. All chapters of the Bible will not have the same richness of Truth for you, but there is no chapter anywhere in the Bible but that will yield some spiritual teaching. A chapter that involves the most thought, oftentimes will yield the greatest teaching.

6. HOW MUCH SHOULD YOU USE THE BIBLE? You should form the habit of reading your Bible every day while you are still in your youth. The daily use of the Bible will give you help, strength, guidance, comfort and faith.

7. ARE THERE ANY OTHER METHODS OF BIBLE STUDY THAN CHAPTER-BY-CHAPTER? There are a number of good study methods. Here are a few:
   [1] OUTLINE STUDY OF EACH BOOK OF THE BIBLE, covering summary of the book, key verse, author, time covered and time of happenings, and the central theme.
   [2] STUDY OF CHRIST, as the key to the Bible as a whole. Before we

understand how the Bible applies to the Church, we should know how it applies to Christ in types, shadows and symbols.

[3] CHARACTER STUDIES. 1 Corinthians 10:11. It is fascinating to study the men and women of the Bible. It has been said: "Men read biography . . . primarily because they live it." The Truths of God are born in our hearts as we study the lives of Bible characters.

[4] STUDY OF DOCTRINE. Take each doctrine of the New Testament Church and trace it through the Bible.

[5] TYPES AND SHADOWS. Study the symbolic illustrations of the Old Testament which give such graphic meaning to Christ and His plan for the Church.

[6] OTHER STUDIES. Word studies, subject studies, prophetic studies. Learn to pray by studying the prayers of the Bible. Let the Holy Spirit lead you. Remember Proverbs 2:3-6.

8. ONE OF THE BIGGEST PROBLEMS OF BIBLE STUDY;
It is possible to know the letter of the Bible and yet not understand nor comprehend its true spiritual meaning. We must seek the Lord's help in interpreting the Bible. John 6:63; 7:16; 5:39, 40.

LESSON 5 STUDY QUESTIONS BASED ON "HOW TO STUDY THE BIBLE"

1. In addition to public Bible instruction, what else will help us know the Truths of God's Word?
2. Where is the best place to begin in reading the whole Bible?
3. Is it necessary to read every chapter?
4. How should I study the Bible — by Books, Chapters or Verses?
5. After reading a chapter, what two things should I have?
6. Should I expect to get something out of every chapter?
7. How much should you use the Bible?
8. Name six methods of Bible study.
9. What is one of the biggest problems of Bible Study?

LESSON 6: SUGGESTIONS ABOUT THE MANNER OF OUR BIBLE STUDY

1. WHAT IS THE BEST TIME FOR THE STUDY OF THE SCRIPTURES?
   It should be at a time that you can have every day.
   It should be at a time when your faculties are keenest.
   It should be at a time when you can have the greatest privacy and quiet.

2. DOES THE BIBLE ITSELF SUGGEST A TIME?
   The Bible emphasizes the morning hours, beginning the day with the Word of God. It gives strength for the day. If we have had our Bible study, nothing that happens during the rest of the day will take it away. Psalms 5:3; Exodus 34:2.

3. HOW MUCH OF THE BIBLE SHALL I READ AT ONE TIME?
   Read until some passage of Scripture really grips your heart! Read at least a chapter — don't be stingy with God's time.

4. WHAT SHOULD BE DONE AFTER BIBLE STUDY?
   Follow your Bible study with MEDITATION; that is, think about what you have read. Ponder, muse, reflect on the things of God. Andrew Murray said, "The intellect gathers and prepares the food upon which we are to feed. In meditation the heart takes it in and feeds on it." Psalms 1:1, 2; 19:14; 119:15, 23, 48, 78, 97, 148; Joshua 1:8; Note Psalms 104:34: "MY meditation of HIM."

5. WHY IS IT IMPORTANT TO MAKE NOTES?
   By using a small notebook or the margin of your Bible, thoughts are clarified into a permanent form. This gives a record of how God has spoken to you day by day, and it also helps refresh your memory concerning things that God has given you. NOTHING WILL ENCOURAGE CAREFUL READING AND MEDITATION more than the recording (in ink) of what we have found from day to day, in our private notebook, or diary, or in the margins of our Bible.

6. IS BIBLE STUDY EASY?
   It is real work to study the Bible. Bible study is the STUDY of the Bible, not dreaming over it, or arguing about it, or defending it. The Bereans SEARCHED the Scriptures (Acts 17:11); Paul says that in dividing the Word of Truth, we are to be WORKMEN (2 Timothy 2:15). Dr. G. Campbell Morgan said: "The Bible yields its treasures to honest toil more readily than does any other serious literature. The Bible never yields to indolence."

7. WHO WILL HELP US IN OUR PERSONAL BIBLE STUDY?
   In addition to the teachers of the church, we have the blessed Holy Spirit Himself who will illuminate the Bible to us. 1 Corinthians 2:11, 12; John 16:13-15; 14:17; 15:26; 1 John 5:6. Children in school have textbooks AND teachers; this is also true in the Church.

8. WHEN GOD SHOWS US SOMETHING IN BIBLE STUDY, HOW CAN WE MAKE IT A PART OF OUR LIVES?

Whatever is revealed will become tremendously real in your life if you will PRAYERFULLY TALK IT OVER WITH GOD. Then, if action is required, do it — believing that God will help you accomplish it.

9. WHAT SHALL I DO IF I FAIL AND MISS IN MY DAILY BIBLE STUDY?

Start again! Even if you have started and failed a dozen times, you can begin again NOW, with a greater longing than ever. Don't allow yourself to become discouraged in your Bible study. Defeat at this point will mean defeat all along the line.

10. WHAT IS THE CROWNING MARK OF THE BIBLE STUDENT?

There are many results from Bible study, but crowning them all is THE JOY OF THE LORD. Psalms 119:162, 14; 19:8; Jeremiah 15:16; John 15:11; Luke 24:25, 27, 32; Acts 8:39; 1 John 1:4.

LESSON 6 STUDY QUESTIONS BASED ON
"SUGGESTIONS ABOUT THE MANNER OF OUR BIBLE STUDY"

1. What is the best time for the study of the Scriptures?
2. Does the Bible itself suggest a time?
3. How much of the Bible shall I read at one time?
4. What should be done after Bible Study?
5. Why is it important to make notes?
6. Is Bible study easy?
7. Who will help us in our personal Bible study?
8. When God shows us something in Bible study, how can we make it a part of our lives?
9. What shall I do if I fail and miss in my daily Bible study?
10. What is the crowning mark of the Bible student?

LESSON 7: THE ATTITUDE OF THE NEW TESTAMENT CHURCH TOWARD THE OLD TESTAMENT PORTION OF THE BIBLE

1. WHAT IS THE OLD TESTAMENT?

    The Old Testament is that portion of the Bible that was written before the coming of Jesus Christ into the world. It is made up of the thirty-nine books which include Genesis through Malachi.

2. WHAT IS A TESTAMENT?

    A testament is an agreement or covenant between two parties; a will, contract. Our Bible has TWO testaments, an old and a new, which show the two great covenants of God with His people.

3. WHAT IS THE NEW TESTAMENT CHURCH?

    The Church that was founded on the teachings of Christ and the Apostles and is dedicated to the New Covenant which Jesus instituted. It is our vision to be a local "New Testament Church." Matthew 16:18, 19.

4. DO NEW TESTAMENT CHURCHES BELIEVE IN THE OLD TESTAMENT?

    Absolutely! Real Christians believe the WHOLE Bible, but interpret the Old Testament portions in the light of God's NEW Testament or Covenant. 2 Timothy 3:14-17.

5. WHAT WAS THE BIBLE OF THE NEW TESTAMENT CHURCH?

    The Old Testament was the only Bible of the Apostles when the Church was first founded; it was the basis of authority for the doctrines and practices of the Apostolic period; the early Church used the Old Testament to prove and verify all that they did. Romans 16:25, 26. The New Testament books developed later and were the written application of the Apostles' use of the Old Testament in teaching the New Covenant.

6. HOW MUCH OF THE OLD TESTAMENT APPLIES TO NEW TESTAMENT CHRISTIANITY?

    All Old Testament teaching and practice should be maintained by the Christian Church UNLESS the New Testament specifically teaches to the contrary. The New Testament's interpretation is the key that unlocks Old Testament teaching. Note Acts 15:28, 29, and also Jesus' use of the Old Testament in the "Sermon on the Mount." Matthew 5, 6 and 7.

7. HERE ARE THREE ILLUSTRATIONS OF THIS PRINCIPLE:

    [1] PRAYER is taught throughout the Bible. In fact, the New Testament uses the Old Testament to teach us about prayer. James 5:16-18.

    [2] EATING PORK was forbidden in the Old Testament, but the New Testament shows that ALL FOOD (except that offered to idols) can be eaten gratefully. Acts 10:14, 15.

    [3] WORSHIP is not cancelled at the Cross. If anything, it is intensified. Acts 24:14; Romans 15:9-12.

8. **DID THE PEOPLE OF OLD TESTAMENT TIMES UNDERSTAND ALL OF THE MEANING OF THE OLD TESTAMENT?**
   No. Much of the deeper spiritual meaning was hidden, especially concerning Christ and His Church. Romans 16:25, 26; 1 Peter 1:12.

9. **IS THE HISTORY OF ISRAEL IN THE OLD TESTAMENT IMPORTANT FOR US TO KNOW?**
   Valuable spiritual lessons can be learned by studying the history of ancient Israel. God uses Israel for an object lesson and direct example to the Church. 1 Corinthians 10:6, 11; 9:9; 10; Romans 4:23, 24; 15:4.

   In addition to the spiritual applications of Israel's history, there are great historical facts that all serious students should know. Ancient history is meaningless apart from the Bible's viewpoint. For instance, the books of Daniel, Ezekiel and Jeremiah give insight to Babylon's history that you will not find in any other textbook.

10. **DO THE END TIMES HOLD ANY SPECIAL PROMISE FOR US?**
    Yes! In the last days there will be greater unfolding of the ancient scriptures. 1 Corinthians 10:11; Daniel 12:4; 1 Peter 1:12.

11. **WHAT WAS JESUS' ATTITUDE TOWARD THE OLD TESTAMENT?**
    Jesus' entire life was to fulfill Scripture. Luke 24:25, 27, 44-48. He accepted the Old Testament as God's inspired record to mankind.

12. **HOW DOES OLD TESTAMENT SCRIPTURE AFFECT JESUS' RETURN?**
    Jesus cannot return to earth before ALL of the prophecies of the Old Testament are fulfilled. Acts 3:21.

13. **IS IT POSSIBLE TO REJECT THE OLD TESTAMENT AND STILL KNOW THE FULNESS OF TRUTH ABOUT THE LORD JESUS CHRIST?**
    No. Acts 10:43; Luke 16:31; John 5:46, 47.

LESSON 7 STUDY QUESTIONS BASED ON
"THE ATTITUDE OF THE NEW TESTAMENT CHURCH"

1. What is the Old Testament?
2. What is a Testament?
3. What is the New Testament Church?
4. Do New Testament Churches believe in the Old Testament?
5. What was the Bible of the New Testament Church?
6. How much of the Old Testament applies to New Testament Christianity?
7. Give three illustrations of this principle.

8. Did the people of Old Testament times understand all of the meaning of the Old Testament?
9. Is the history of Israel in the Old Testament important for us to know?
10. Do the end times hold any special promise for us?
11. What was Jesus' attitude toward the Old Testament?
12. How does Old Testament Scripture affect Jesus' return?
13. Is it possible to reject the Old Testament and still know the Truth about Jesus Christ?

PART II.
GOD, ANGELS AND MAN

PART II. GOD, ANGELS AND MAN

PART II. GOD, ANGELS AND MAN

LESSON 1: THE NATURE OF GOD

1. IS IT POSSIBLE TO UNDERSTAND GOD?

   One of the prevailing ideas among Christians is that none may know or understand God. We are told, so very often, that God is incomprehensible, that He dwells in High and Holy State, unapproachable by His creatures, and that it is impossible for finite man to understand the infinite God. JUST THE REVERSE IS TRUE! God has, in Jesus Christ, made Himself one of us, brought Himself down to our level, touched our humanity, carried our infirmities, and borne all the stain of our sin.

   The Bible was written with the specific purpose of giving to every believer a complete revelation and understanding of the God he loves. "That we may KNOW HIM" is the purpose of its truth. Take advantage, then, of the infinite side of your own nature to understand the nature and being of an infinite God. Philippians 3:10; Hosea 6:3.

2. WHO IS GOD?

   God is the Supreme Being who is wise enough, able enough and strong enough to create and maintain ALL THINGS. Genesis 1; Nehemiah 9:6; Psalms 24:1, 2; 33:6, 7, 9; 65:6; 1 Timothy 1:17; Acts 17:22-31; Revelation 10:6.

3. WHAT DO WE MEAN WHEN WE SAY THAT GOD IS "INFINITE"?

   God is INFINITE because He is UNLIMITED. Nothing happens that He does not allow; nothing happens that He does not know about. Nothing can put a boundary around God, such as time, space, etc. 1 Kings 8:27; Job 37:5, 23; Psalms 147:5; Isaiah 40:28; Jeremiah 23:24.

4. WHAT DOES THE WORD "GOD" MEAN?

   The word "God" is a title that men use to describe this supreme, infinite being. The Bible recognizes only ONE God as actually existing, but the heathen often recognize other things by this title. 1 Corinthians 8:4-6.

5. IS IT POSSIBLE TO KNOW GOD THROUGH NATURE ALONE?

   No. While the power and magnitude of this great God is seen in the created universe, the real understanding of His nature and attributes only comes through the study of His Word, the Bible. Psalms 138:2.

6. HAS GOD ALWAYS EXISTED?

   Yes. Before time began, God already existed. This is another way of saying that God is ETERNAL; that is, having no beginning or ending. "From everlasting to everlasting, thou art God" – Psalms 90:1-2. Actually, God is SELF-EXISTENT. He is life in Himself. Genesis 1:1; Isaiah 41:4; 44:6; Psalms 36:9. Note Exodus 3:2; John 1:4, "In Him was life."

31

7. WHAT IS GOD MADE OF?

"God is a Spirit" (John 4:24), which means that He is a living, personal being without a visible form. Think of all the living creatures you know about: fish, birds, animals and men. God lives just as they do — WITH ONE GREAT EXCEPTION! Since all MATTER is subject to change and death, God chose to be without form, invisible, and, therefore, able to be everywhere at once! God is a personal being, but without flesh and blood which can be affected by death.

"God is a Spirit" — John 4:24.
"The invisible things of Him (God)" — Romans 1:20.
"Now the Lord is that Spirit" — 2 Corinthians 3:17.
"Him who is invisible" — Hebrews 11:27.
"No man hath seen God at any time" — John 1:18.

8. HOW BIG IS GOD?

God's bigness is UNLIMITED. He is bigger than the entire universe, larger than anyone can realize. There is no device known to man by which God's bigness can be measured. Note again question 3 about the word "infinite." His hands are large enough to measure the waters. He can weigh the mountains in His scales. He covers all. Isaiah 40:12, 15, 22.

9. WHERE IS GOD?

God's throne and home is in heaven; yet, it can be said that God inhabits the whole earth and is <u>everywhere</u>. Isaiah 66:1; 2 Chronicles 16:9; Proverbs 15:3; Psalms 139:7, 8.

10. TWELVE DESCRIPTIONS THAT HELP US UNDERSTAND THE INFINITE GOD:

[1] ETERNAL — Unlimited by time.
"the everlasting God" — Genesis 21:33.

[2] UNCHANGING — Unaffected by circumstances, immutable.
"I am the Lord, I change not" — Malachi 3:6.

[3] OMNIPOTENT — All powerful.
"I am the almighty God" — Genesis 17:1.

[4] OMNISCIENT — All knowing.
"God . . . knoweth all things" — 1 John 3:20.

[5] OMNIPRESENT — Unlimited by space, He is everywhere.
"Do I not fill heaven and earth? Saith the Lord" — Jeremiah 23:24.

[6] HOLY — Absolutely pure; sinless and hating sin.
"I the Lord your God am holy" — Leviticus 19:2.

32

[7] JUST — Fair and impartial; truth is the basis of His righteousness.
"A God of truth and without iniquity, just and right is He" —
Deuteronomy 32:4.

[8] FAITHFUL — Absolutely trustworthy; He keeps His Word.
"He abideth faithful: He cannot deny Himself" — 2 Timothy 2:13.

[9] BENEVOLENT — Good, kind, desiring our welfare.
"The Lord is good to all" — Psalms 145:9.

[10] MERCIFUL — Full of pity.
"The Lord . . . merciful . . . keeping mercy" — Exodus 34:6, 7.

[11] GRACIOUS — Showing undeserved kindness, forgiving.
"I will hear; for I am gracious" — Exodus 22:27.

[12] LOVE
"God is love" — 1 John 4:8.

LESSON 1 STUDY QUESTIONS BASED ON "THE NATURE OF GOD"

1. Is it possible to understand God?
2. Who is God?
3. What do we mean when we say that God is "infinite"?
4. What does the word "god" mean?
5. Is it possible to know God through nature alone?
6. Has God always existed?
7. What is God made of?
8. How big is God?
9. Where is God?
10. List twelve descriptions that help us understand the infinite God.

LESSON 2: THE FULLNESS OF THE GODHEAD

1. **WHAT MYSTERY CONCERNING GOD DOES THE BIBLE REVEAL?**
   The Bible reveals to us the mystery that in the makeup of the ONE true God there is the Father, the Son and the Holy Spirit, and that these THREE are ONE. Matthew 3:16, 17; 1 Timothy 3:16; Colossians 1:26.

2. **IS IT POSSIBLE FOR US TO UNDERSTAND THE "MYSTERY" OF THE GODHEAD?**
   "Mystery" is defined by Webster as: "Something that has not been, or cannot be, explained, hence, something beyond human comprehension." Although God is a mystery, we can gain a satisfactory understanding of Him through the statements of the Bible and the inspiration of the Holy Spirit. 1 Corinthians 2:6-14. Our finite intelligence is inadequate to explain human life, let alone the makeup of the infinite God; however, our minds are capable of accepting, believing and experiencing the God that is revealed in the Bible.

3. **ARE THERE THREE GODS OR ONE GOD?**
   There is but ONE God, and He is three-fold in personality. 2 Corinthians 13:14; Matthew 28:19; 1 Corinthians 12:4, 5, 6; 1 Timothy 2:5.

4. **"THE GREAT CONFESSION OF ISRAEL" EMPHASIZES THE ONENESS OF GOD:**
   "Hear, O Israel: The LORD our God is one LORD" — Deuteronomy 6:4.

5. **WHAT IS MEANT BY GOD'S ONENESS?**
   The oneness of God is not numerical in meaning, but rather refers to God's UNITY. 1 John 5:7; John 1:1; Colossians 2:9; Ephesians 1:2, 3.

6. **ARE THERE BIBLE REFERENCES THAT PROVE THAT GOD IS A UNITY, RATHER THAN JUST A "NUMBER ONE" GOD?**
   Yes, here are a few illustrations:

   [1] "Elohim," the most common Hebrew word for God (as in Genesis 1:1), is a PLURAL noun.

   [2] Genesis 1:26 — "God said let us . . . ."

   [3] Genesis 3:22 — "Behold the man is become as one of us."

   [4] Genesis 11:7 — "Let us go down, and . . . confound their language."

   [5] Ecclesiastes 12:1 — "Remember now thy creators" (Literal translation)

   [6] Psalms 149:2 — "Let Israel rejoice in his makers" (Hebrew in plural).

   [7] 1 Thessalonians 1:1; Ephesians 1:17; 2:18; Revelation 1:4, 5; 3:21; Matthew 3:16, 17.

7. THERE IS A DIFFERENCE BETWEEN <u>WHAT</u> GOD IS AND <u>WHO</u> GOD IS.
   When we speak of WHAT God is we refer to His NATURE or ATTRIBUTES
   (as in Lesson 1); WHO God is refers to His personal makeup and name, and
   this is the subject of Lessons 2 and 3.

A NATURE is WHAT someone
or something is.

A PERSON is WHO someone is.

8. THE GOD OF THE BIBLE IS NOT:

	BUT HE IS:	AS:
1 God in 3 Gods;	1 God with	John 15:26
1 Nature in 3 Natures;	1 Nature in	Galatians 4:6
1 Person in 3 Persons;	3 Persons;	Ephesians 2:18

9. WHEN WE REACH HEAVEN WILL WE SEE GOD AS THREE OR ONE?
   We will see the three personalities of God — the Father, the Son, and the
   Holy Spirit — wonderfully and mysteriously blended into one unity. A man
   may be a father, a son, and a husband all at one time, but he is viewed as
   one man. In similar manner, we shall see the Godhead as one God. It is
   interesting to note Stephen's experience in Acts 7:55; also, John's experience
   in Revelation 1:4, fourth and fifth chapters.

10. WHAT IS THE MAIN REASON THAT PEOPLE MISUNDERSTAND THE
    GODHEAD?
    Most people do not realize that the God of the Bible is both VISIBLE and
    INVISIBLE! With the visible manifestation of His being we are well
    acquainted; the Lord Jesus Christ is the visible Word or expression of God.
    However, there are also two INVISIBLE entities, even the Father and the
    blessed Holy Spirit. John 1:1, 14; 1 John 1:1-3; Colossians 2:9.

11. IS THERE ANYTHING THAT CAN ILLUSTRATE THIS TRUTH?
    Yes, man himself. While man is positively body, soul and spirit, it is the
    BODY alone that is VISIBLE. The soul and spirit are invisible, yet they are
    none the less real and necessary to the revelation of the complete man!

12. WHAT IS THE SIGNIFICANCE OF THE WORD "TRINITY"?
    The word "Trinity" is not in the Bible, and for that reason we are not
    using it in our teaching, even though it is a very proper word to use in the

35

explanation of the THREEness of the Godhead. The word Trinity simply means "the union of Three in One," and may be applied to either God or man, for both are "triune" in their being. God as Father, Son and Holy Spirit; and man as body, soul and spirit. ONE IS BUILT IN THE LIKENESS AND IMAGE OF THE OTHER!

13. WHAT WORD FROM THE BIBLE CAN BE USED TO ILLUSTRATE GOD'S TRI-UNITY?

While the word "Trinity" is not in the Bible, the word "THREE" is. There is no revelation of the Godhead throughout the entire Bible which does not carry the seal and the impress of the THREE. 1 John 5:7.

14. SOME IMPORTANT THOUGHTS ON "THE FULLNESS OF THE GODHEAD."

The Godhead is THREE in operation and manifestation, but definitely ONE in purpose, power and essence. It is important to note that the entities which comprise the Godhead have certain distinctive attributes WHICH NEVER CHANGE, yet "These Three are One." 1 John 5:7.

[1] GOD THE FATHER: The Creator, the Controller, the Planner, the Great Architect of the universe. Dwelling in Glory and Light which is physically unapproachable, the Father exists as the Absolute, the Self-existing, the Unapproachable One, the great Uncaused Cause of all things. For 2,000 years, from Adam to Abraham, the personality of the Father dominates the scene of redemptive operations.

[2] GOD THE SON: The incarnated eternal WORD; the living flesh and bone manifestation of divinity to humanity. His personality is seen typically in the sacrificial BLOOD dispensation from Abraham to the Cross, 2,000 years. Revealed as a Lamb to take away sin — as a Lion to subdue all things.

[3] GOD THE HOLY SPIRIT: The Inspiration, the Quickening Power of the Church. The invisible Presence of God that acts as teacher, guide and comforter. God's anointing power and sanctifying INFLUENCE. The Revelator of the "things of Christ." He is revealed in this present Church Age of 2,000 years.

LESSON 2 STUDY QUESTIONS BASED ON
"THE FULLNESS OF THE GODHEAD"

1. What mystery concerning God does the Bible reveal?
2. Is it possible for us to understand the "mystery" of the Godhead?
3. Are there three Gods or one God?
4. What is "The Great Confession of Israel" and what does it emphasize?
5. What is meant by God's oneness?

LESSON 2 STUDY QUESTIONS BASED ON
"THE FULLNESS OF THE GODHEAD" (Continued)

6. List seven Bible references proving that God is a unity.
7. Explain the difference between WHAT God is and WHO God is.
8. Why do people misunderstand the Godhead?
9. How do you think God will appear in Heaven?
10. Illustrate and explain the Tri-Unity of the Godhead.

LESSON 3: TYPES WHICH ILLUSTRATE THE GODHEAD

GOD

		FATHER	SON	HOLY SPIRIT
1.	HIS NAME	THE LORD	JESUS	CHRIST
2.	Heavenly Bodies	The Sun	The Moon	The Stars
3.	Noah's Ark Genesis 6:14-22	Foundation	2nd Story with Door	Upper Story with Window
4.	The Patriarchs Genesis 12–50	Abraham	Isaac	Jacob
5.	Gate of Eden Genesis 3:24	Cherub	Flaming Sword	Cherub
6.	Primary Colors	Yellow	Red	Blue
7.	Lid of the Ark Exodus 25:10	Cherub	Mercy Seat	Cherub
8.	Ark's Contents Exodus 25:21	Law	Manna Exodus 16:33	Fruitful Rod
9.	The Vail Exodus 26	Inwrought Cherub	Vail Itself	Inwrought Cherub
10.	High Priest Exodus 28:1-30	Urim ("Lights")	High Priest	Thummim ("Perfections")
11.	Tab. Coverings Exodus 36:18-19	Badger Skins	Ram Skins— Red	Goats' Hair
12.	Bringing Water Exodus 17:5-7	Rod	Rock	Living Waters
13.	Cleansing Leper Lev. 14:12-29	Blood & Oil On Right Ear	Thumb	Great Toe
14.	Angels Genesis 18:6	Angel	Angel	Angel
15.	Tabernacle Book of Exodus	Outer Court	Holy Place	Most Holy Place
16.	Jesus' Baptism Luke 3:21	Voice of Father	Jesus in Water	Spirit as Dove
17.	Three Loaves Luke 11:5	One Loaf	2nd Loaf	3rd Loaf
18.	Matthew 28:19	Father	Son	Holy Spirit
19.	2 Corinthians 13:4	Love of God	Grace of Lord Jesus Christ	Communion of Holy Ghost
20.	1 Corinthians 12:4, 5, 6	Same God	Same Lord	Same Spirit
21.	1 John 5:7	The Father	The Word	The Holy Ghost
22.	Ephesians 2:18	Unto the Father	Through Him	By One Spirit
23.	Man's Makeup	Soul	Body	Spirit

LESSON 3 STUDY QUESTIONS BASED ON
"TYPES WHICH ILLUSTRATE THE GODHEAD"

1. Can you list at least twelve of the twenty-three types given on the chart which illustrate the three-fold nature of the Godhead?

LESSON 4: WHAT IS THE NAME OF GOD?

1. WHAT DOES THE WORD "GOD" MEAN?
   The word "God" is a title which means "one who is worshipped." 1 Corinthians 8:5, 6.

2. WHY SHOULD THE TRUE GOD HAVE A NAME?
   The Name of God establishes the identity of God and separates Him from heathen dieties. Man is enabled to address God properly through His Name. Genesis 32:24-30; Exodus 3:13-14; Judges 13.

3. THE ANCIENT HEBREWS BELIEVED THAT GOD AND HIS NAME WERE THE SAME!
   This means that God and His Name were inseparable; all that the true God stood for was invested in His Name. His Name and His person were the same.

4. WHO WAS THE FIRST MAN TO RECEIVE THE REVELATION OF GOD'S NAME?
   Moses, as recorded in Exodus 3:13-14.

5. HOW WAS GOD KNOWN BEFORE MOSES' TIME?
   Apparently He was known as "The true God" or "God Almighty." Exodus 6:3.

6. WHAT WAS THE NAME THAT GOD GAVE TO MOSES?
   The Hebrew word is composed of four letters (יהוה, JHVH), so it is called the "Tetragrammaton" (the four-lettered name).

7. WHAT DOES THIS FOUR-LETTERED HEBREW NAME MEAN?
   The Tetragrammaton means "I AM" — just as it is translated in your Bible. Exodus 3:14.

8. HOW MANY TIMES DOES THIS NAME APPEAR IN THE HEBREW BIBLE?
   This is the most frequent Name of God in the Scriptures. It appears 6,823 times in the Hebrew Old Testament.

9. DID ISRAELITES EVER PRONOUNCE THIS NAME?
   No, for it was considered too sacred. Leviticus 24:16 shows that just to utter the Name was punishable with death by stoning.

10. WHAT DID AN ISRAELITE USE FOR GOD'S NAME — IF HE COULDN'T PRONOUNCE OR UTTER THE ORIGINAL JHVH?
    He used a substituted word; which is Adonai in Hebrew, Kurios in Greek and Lord in English. The ancient rabbis put the vowel marks of Adonai on the original JHVH to remind them to pronounce Adonai rather than God's actual Name.

11. WHERE DID THE WORD "JEHOVAH" COME FROM?
    The word "Jehovah" came into being in 1520 A.D., and is another way of

referring to the original JHVH. The translators combined the vowel points of "e," "o" and "a" (which had been placed upon the JHVH to remind the Jews to say Adonai) with the JHVH; thus, they came up with the word JeHoVaH. Jewish encyclopedias identify the Name "Jehovah" as a hybrid word and unacceptable as an authentic revelation of God's Name. Naturally "Jehovah" couldn't have been used by Jesus or the early Church because IT WASN'T EVEN A WORD AT THAT TIME!

12. DO YOU KNOW WHY THE CAPITALIZED WORD "LORD" APPEARS IN THE KING JAMES VERSION OF THE OLD TESTAMENT?

Whenever you find "LORD" in the Old Testament (capitalized), it means that the original Hebrew text uses the Tetragrammaton in that particular place.

13. THEREFORE, THE OLD TESTAMENT SHOWS US THAT THE NAME OF GOD THE FATHER IS "LORD"!

[1] Exodus 15:3 – "The LORD is a man of war: the LORD is His Name."
[2] Isaiah 42:8 – "I am the LORD: that is my Name . . . ."
[3] Jeremiah 33:2 – "Thus saith the Lord the maker thereof, the LORD that formed it, to establish it; the LORD is His Name."
[4] Jeremiah 16:21 – ". . . and they shall know that my Name is The LORD."
[5] Amos 5:8; 9:6 – "The LORD is His Name."

14. THE GOD OF THE OLD TESTAMENT REVEALS HIMSELF THROUGH JESUS AS THE GREAT "I AM":

[1] John 4:25, 26 – "I that speak unto thee am He" or "I AM that speaketh . . . ."
[2] John 8:23 - "I AM from above . . . I AM not of this World."
[3] John 8:24 - ". . . for if ye believe not that I AM he . . . ."
[4] John 8:58 – "before Abraham was, I AM."
[5] John 13:19 – "that . . . ye may believe that I AM."
[6] John 18:5 – "Jesus saith unto them, I AM he . . . ."
[7] Matthew 14:27 – "Be of good cheer; it is I (I AM); be not afraid."
[8] Mark 14:61, 62 – "Art thou . . .? And Jesus said, I AM."

15. NOTICE HOW JESUS DESCRIBES HIMSELF AS THE GREAT "I AM."

It was this claim of Diety that sent Jesus to the cross. He fearlessly employed I AM (ego eimi, the Greek emphatic usage) in describing Himself. HE DECLARED THAT "I AM":

[1] The Bread of Life – John 6:35.
[2] The Light of the World – John 8:12.
[3] The Door of the Sheep – John 10:7.
[4] The Good Shepherd – John 10:11.

    [5] The Resurrection and the Life — John 11:25.

    [6] The Way, Truth and the Life — John 14:6.

    [7] The True Vine — John 15:1.

    [8] Alpha and Omega, Beginning and End, Revelation 1:8.

16. GOD HATH MADE JESUS BOTH LORD AND CHRIST — Acts 2:36.

Jesus refers over 100 times in John's Gospel to God as His Father. In the New Testament Christians also refer to God as Father, and NEVER invoke Him through His personal Name of LORD. The reason is obvious! The Father gave His Name of LORD to JESUS. In addition, the Holy Spirit anointed Him, making Him CHRIST as well. We, therefore, use the Name of the LORD Jesus Christ — the Name which reveals the fullness of the Godhead Bodily — the Father, and the Son and the Holy Spirit. A TRI-UNITY GOD revealed through a TRI-UNITY NAME!

17. HERE ARE ADDITIONAL REFERENCES SHOWING JESUS WAS MADE LORD:

John 5:43;· Luke 2:11; Acts 2:36; Romans 10:9; 2 Corinthians 4:5; Ephesians 4:5; 1 Corinthians 8:6; 12:3; Philippians 2:11; Ephesians 3:11; Philippians 3:8; 1 Corinthians 15:31; Acts 7:59, 60; 9:5; 9:17; 22:8-12; Mark 16:19.

Note Paul's opening salutations: 1 Corinthians 1:3; 2 Corinthians 1:2, 3; Galatians 1:3; etc. He mentions God as FATHER, then adds significantly "The Lord Jesus Christ."

WATER BAPTISM in the Name of the Father, and of the Son and of the Holy Spirit finds wonderful fulfillment in "The LORD-Jesus-Christ." Acts 2:38; 8:16; 10:48; 19:5; 22:17.

18. WHAT IS THE NAME OF GOD FOR OUR DAY?

The Lord Jesus Christ. Acts 16:31.

LESSON 4 STUDY QUESTIONS BASED ON "WHAT IS THE NAME OF GOD?"

1.   What does the word "God" mean?

2.   Why should the true God have a name?

3.   The ancient Hebrews believed what about God and His Name?

4.   Who was the first man to receive the revelation of God's Name?

5.   How was God known before Moses' time?

6.   What was the Name that God gave to Moses?

7.   What does the four-lettered Hebrew Name mean?

LESSON 4 STUDY QUESTIONS BASED ON
"WHAT IS THE NAME OF GOD?" (Continued)

8. How many times does this Name appear in the Hebrew Bible?
9. Did Israelites ever pronounce this Name?
10. What did an Israelite use for God's Name?
11. Where did the word "Jehovah" come from?
12. Why is "LORD" capitalized in the King James Old Testament?
13. Can you give three references that show that the Name of the Father is LORD?
14. Name four of the eight references revealing Jesus as the great "I AM."
15. Jesus made eight statements about himself being the "I AM." Name them.
16. What is the meaning of Acts 2:36?
17. Can you name other references declaring that Jesus was made Lord?
18. What is the Name of God for our day?

LESSON 5: THE HEAVENLY HOSTS, A STUDY OF ANGELS

1. **WHAT DOES THE WORD "ANGEL" MEAN?**

    The word "angel" simply means "messenger." In the Bible this term refers to any of three categories: [1] A spiritual, heavenly creature that is part of the heavenly hosts; [2] Sometimes the term applies to God Himself (Genesis 22:11-15); [3] And it is a term that can apply to men with ministries (as church pastors, Revelation 1:20; 2:1).

2. **WHAT IS A HEAVENLY ANGEL?**

    An angel is a heavenly messenger that can provide us with actual physical help to accomplish God's will. An angel can appear with physical form or voice or be invisible. Hebrews 1:14 calls them "ministering spirits."

3. **THE BIBLE CLASSIFIES THREE TYPES OF HEAVENLY BEINGS, ALL OF WHICH ARE USUALLY CALLED ANGELS.**

    [1]   Seraph or Seraphim.

    [2]   Cherub or Cherubim.

    [3]   Angel or Angels.

4. **WHAT ARE THE SERAPHIM?**

    The seraphim are mentioned only once in the Bible, Isaiah 6. The meaning of the root word is "to consume with fire." Little is said about them in explanation. We know there are more than one; that they are the only creatures in Scripture possessing six wings; that they are very close to God and are deeply associated with His holiness; they are very powerful; and they do have a ministry to men on earth.

5. **HERE IS ONE INTERPRETATION OF WHO THE SERAPHIM ARE!**

    It is our conviction that the "living creatures" mentioned in Revelation 4:8 are one and the same as the Seraphim mentioned in Isaiah 6. We feel that these four are men who have conquered death itself and stand before God, angels and mankind with the irrefutable argument that death has been conquered FOUR times in past history: [1] ENOCH, translated during the Patriarchal Age. [2] MOSES, resurrected during the Law Period. [3] ELIJAH, translated during the time of the Prophets. [4] JESUS, resurrected at the opening of the New Covenant. Note that two died and were raised to eternal life; two did not die at all, but were translated. Assurance is hereby given to all who have died in Christ and we who remain alive until His coming.

6. **WHAT ARE THE CHERUBIM?**

    Inside the tabernacle of Moses, the pictured heavenly beings are always cherubim. Apparently they have only one pair of wings, and are mentioned many times in the Bible. Note that the Living Creatures of Ezekiel have four wings and are called cherubim.

7. **WHAT IS THE MOST IMPORTANT MINISTRY OF THE CHERUBIM?**

   Genesis 3:24 shows the cherubim guarding the tree of Life and keeping sinful man out. They are also seen in the tabernacle, guarding the ark and keeping sinful man from entering. Exodus 26:31.

8. **WHO ARE THE THREE NAMED HEAVENLY DIGNITARIES?**

   [1] LUCIFER, whose name means "day star," also called Satan or the Devil. Revelation 12: 9; Isaiah 14:12.

   [2] MICHAEL, whose name means "Who is like God," was the warrior archangel who appeared whenever there was war or impending battle. Revelation 12:7; Daniel 10:13-21, 12:1; Jude 9.

   [3] GABRIEL, whose name means "God is mighty," was God's messenger who carried Divine communications to men. Luke 1:19, 26; Daniel 8:16; 9:21; 10:10-21.

LESSON 5 STUDY QUESTIONS BASED ON "THE HEAVENLY HOSTS, A STUDY OF ANGELS"

1. What does the word "angel" mean?
2. What is a heavenly angel?
3. What are the three types of heavenly beings mentioned in the Bible?
4. What are the seraphim?
5. What is one interpretation of who they are?
6. Who are the cherubim?
7. What is the most important ministry of the cherubim?
8. Who are the three named heavenly dignitaries?

LESSON 6: SOME INTERESTING FACTS ABOUT ANGELS

1. THE CHURCH WILL JUDGE ANGELS.
    1 Corinthians 6:3. Some people are always looking for angels. Esteem them, but do not overestimate their importance.

2. SATAN CAN TRANSFORM HIMSELF INTO AN ANGEL OF LIGHT.
    2 Corinthians 11:14. Do not, therefore, seek angels — you could be misled.

3. HELL WAS BUILT FOR THE DEVIL AND HIS ANGELS, NOT FOR MAN.
    Matthew 25:41. When men refuse Christ, they automatically go where the rebellious angels are consigned.

4. THE CHURCH HAS BEEN GIVEN COMPLETE AUTHORITY OVER ALL FALLEN ANGELS (INCLUDING SATAN), DEATH AND HELL.
    Luke 10:17-20.

5. ANGELS DO NOT UNDERSTAND SALVATION AND CANNOT TEACH IT.
    1 Peter 1:12; Acts 10:3-6.

6. EVEN A HEAVENLY ANGEL COULD LEAD YOU ASTRAY!
    Galatians 1:8 notes that even an angel of heaven could mislead. This shows the supreme importance of knowing God's Word.

7. ANGELS ARE "MINISTERING SPIRITS" TO THE REDEEMED.
    They are our protectors. There is a tremendous relationship that exists between a Christian's activities and the ministry of the angel that is given to him. Matthew 18:10; 1 Corinthians 11:10; Mark 1:13; Hebrews 1:14; 1 Kings 19:5-7; Luke 22:43; Acts 12:7.

8. ANGELS KNOW THE NAMES OF CHRISTIANS WHO WITNESS.
    The angels will know the witnessing saint when he gets to heaven! Luke 12:8. Note also that fallen angels ("evil spirits") recognize the authority of the saints, even when they are not present. Acts 19:15.

9. ANGELS WATCH THE REJOICING OF GOD OVER A SINNER'S REPEN-TANCE.
    Luke 15:10. The Bible does NOT say that the angels rejoice, but rather they are in the presence of God's rejoicing!

10. ANGELS CARRIED LAZARUS TO PARADISE AND WILL BE USED IN THE LAST DAYS TO GATHER GOD'S ELECT.
    Luke 16:22; Matthew 24:31.

11. ANGELS DO NOT KNOW WHEN THE SECOND COMING WILL BE.
    Matthew 24:36.

12. WE ARE FORBIDDEN TO WORSHIP ANGELS.
    Colossians 2:18; Revelation 22:8-9.

13. ANGELS DO NOT RULE THE WORLD TO COME — WE DO!
    Hebrews 2:5.

14. DO NOT SPEAK LIGHTLY OF THE DEVIL, FOR HE STILL IS AN ANGELIC DIGNITARY.
    Jude 9. Though Michael was on the same level as Lucifer, he did not make any foolish charges or accusations.

15. ANGELS DO NOT UNDERSTAND GRACE, ONLY LAW.
    Hebrews 2:2; Galatians 3:19; Acts 7:53; 1 Corinthians 11:10; Exodus 23:20 and 21.

16. ANGELS CANNOT SEPARATE US FROM THE LOVE OF GOD.
    Romans 8:38, 39.

LESSON 6 STUDY QUESTIONS BASED ON "SOME INTERESTING FACTS ABOUT ANGELS"

1. Who will someday judge angels?
2. Who can transform himself into an angel of light?
3. Was hell built for man?
4. How much authority does the Church have over fallen angels?
5. Why can't an angel replace a teacher in the Church?
6. Is it safe to follow a heavenly angel's advice?
7. What do we mean by saying that angels are "ministering spirits"?
8. How can a Christian become known in the Heavenlies?
9. How do angels know when a sinner repents?
10. How did Lazarus get to Paradise?
11. Do the angels know when Jesus' Second Coming to Earth will be?
12. Is it all right to worship angels?
13. Who will rule the world to come?
14. Is it all right to speak foolish accusations against the Devil?
15. Why do angels understand law, but not grace?
16. Can a powerful angel separate us from the love of God?

LESSON 7: THE FALL OF LUCIFER AND A BLIGHTED WORLD

1. **WHO WAS LUCIFER?**
    Lucifer was the highest angel in heaven. He was the anointed cherub of God that had access to the throne of God. He was chiefest among the angels of heaven. He was called the "Son of the Morning." Read Ezekiel 28:12-14.

2. **WHAT DID LUCIFER LOOK LIKE?**
    Lucifer was a most beautiful creature. Every precious stone was his covering. When he spoke it sounded like a great pipe organ. He was perfect in beauty and in wisdom. Ezekiel 28:13, 14, 15.

3. **WHAT HAPPENED TO LUCIFER?**
    Iniquity was found in him (basically pride), and he attempted to overthrow the throne of God and take God's place. God threw him and all his followers out of heaven. They became the Devil and his demons. Notice how God challenges the five boastful "I will's" of Satan with five "I will" statements of His own! Ezekiel 28:17; Isaiah 14:12-14.

4. **WHEN DID GOD FIRST CREATE THE HEAVENS AND THE EARTH?**
    In the beginning of time, God made the heavens and the earth. When this beginning was, we do not know and the Bible does not say. Science says it happened millions of years ago. Genesis 1:1.

5. **WHAT HAPPENED TO THE EARTH?**
    After God's perfect creation the earth suffered a terrible upheaval that caused it to become without form and void. Genesis 1:2.

6. **WHAT WAS THE CAUSE OF THIS TERRIBLE UPHEAVAL THAT DESTROYED THE EARTH?**
    The fall of Lucifer and his angel followers caused this terrible upheaval in the world. When they were thrown from heaven, the world was turned upside down and all was without form and void. Isaiah 14:16, 17; 24:1; Jeremiah 4:23-26.

7. **WHO FELL FROM HEAVEN WITH LUCIFER?**
    A great host of angels who sinned with Lucifer fell from heaven with him. Jude 6; 2 Peter 2:4.

8. **WHERE ARE LUCIFER AND HIS DEMONS NOW?**
    Apparently, the Devil and his angels have the ability to roam the earth day and night at will; however, they are chained by the curse of darkness and reserved to final judgment. Matthew 12:43-45; Jude 6; Job 1:7; Revelation 12:9 (yet future); 1 Peter 5:8; 9; Matthew 8:28-34; Mark 7:7, 10; Note Luke 8:31.

9. **WHEN DID THE PRESENT WORLD'S CREATION TAKE PLACE?**
    The present earth with its various orders of life was created in six days. We

do not know when this actually happened, except that it began after "the Spirit of God moved upon the face of the waters." Genesis 1:2.

10. DID GOD ACTUALLY CREATE EVERYTHING IN THE PRESENT WORLD IN SIX DAYS, OR IS THAT JUST A MANNER OF SPEECH?

The simplest explanation is that each day was a 24-hour day, based on the repeated expression, "And the evening and the morning were the____day." Genesis 1:5, 8, 13, 19, 23 and 31. Some feel that each day was actually a period of time, such as a thousand years as mentioned in 2 Peter 3:8. The advent of the "space age" has made us all aware of the new dimensions in time and space that have opened to the thinking of man. Also, it should be noted that even here on earth "a day" has various meanings, depending on whether you live in the Arctic, the Equator or elsewhere. The main thought of the first chapter of the Bible is that God Almighty created the earth and its various forms of life in an ordered, logical way. He could have done this in any number of ways. The purpose of this chapter is not to give a scientific treatise on creation, but rather a simple historical account of creation that would be satisfactory and acceptable to all races of men for a period of approximately 6,000 years.

11. WHAT IS THE "THEORY OF EVOLUTION"?

The unproved idea that all things have evolved, or developed, in the course of long ages, from simple forms to more complex forms. This THEORY contradicts the Bible account of the creation. Note the expression, "After their kind" in Genesis 1:21, 24, 25. God made each "kind" of life distinctly different!

LESSON 7 STUDY QUESTIONS BASED ON
"THE FALL OF LUCIFER AND A BLIGHTED WORLD"

1. Who was Lucifer?
2. What did Lucifer look like?
3. What happened to Lucifer?
4. When did God first create the heavens and the earth?
5. What happened to the earth?
6. What was the cause of this terrible upheaval that destroyed the earth?
7. Who fell from heaven with Lucifer?
8. Where are Lucifer and his demons now?
9. When did the present world's creation take place?
10. Did God actually create everything in the world in six literal days?
11. What is the "Theory of Evolution"?

LESSON 8: THE CREATION OF MAN AND THE APPEARANCE OF SIN

1. WHICH IS THE PRINCIPAL CREATURE ON EARTH?

   The principal creature on earth is man because in the beginning God Himself especially formed his body, gave him a rational soul, made him ruler over the earth, and — above all — created him in His image. Genesis 2:7; 1:26, 27.

2. WHO WAS THE FIRST MAN?

   His name was Adam. Genesis 1 and 2; 1 Corinthians 15:45. He did not evolve from monkeys, but was the result of an immediate creation by God.

3. DOES THE BIBLE TEACH THAT ADAM WAS CREATED 4,000 B.C.?

   Many people think this because of the dates given in the margin of their Bible. Usually, these dates are based on Ussher's Chronology, which in turn is based on a study of the geneologies of the Bible. The geneologies of the Bible indicate that Adam's SIN did take place about 4,000 B.C., but not his CREATION. Adam undoubtedly was created long before his sin, and had children other than Cain, Abel and Seth. Consider that God told him to reproduce while he was still without sin. Genesis 1:28. This he must have done, which would account for the obvious presence of other people on the earth at that time. Genesis 4:16, 17.

4. WHAT WAS THE IMAGE OF GOD?

   It means to be like God — in actions, appearance, thought, etc. It meant that man was able to enjoy the spiritual perfection of God, and to possess it by deliberate choice. Colossians 3:10; Ephesians 4:24; Hebrews 1:3; 6:1; Ephesians 4:12, 13.

5. DOES MAN STILL BEAR THE IMAGE OF GOD?

   Man lost the image of God (perfection) when he fell into sin. In Christians a restoration of this image is taking place through the work of the Holy Spirit. The full restoration will be completed in the resurrection. Genesis 5:3; 1 Corinthians 15:52-54; Psalms 17:15.

6. IS MAN A SPIRIT BEING?

   Man is more of a spirit being than he is a physical being. There is a spirit in man, inbreathed by God, by which he has a far greater capacity for eternal things and for the spiritual realm, than for the temporal things and the material realm. Proverbs 20:27; 1 Corinthians 2:11.

7. HOW MANY PARTS ARE THERE IN A MAN?

   Man is three-fold, just as God is a tri-unity. Man is a spirit, soul and body. 1 Thessalonians 5:23. Our BODY is fed by natural food; our SOUL (the seat of our affections) is fed by love; and our SPIRIT is fed by the inspired Word of God. Genesis 1:26; Job 32:8; Ecclesiastes 3:11; Matthew 4:4.

8. HOW WAS WOMAN CREATED?

   Woman was created by God out of a rib which the Lord removed from

50

Adam's side. Genesis 2:21-22.

9. **WHY WAS WOMAN CREATED?**

God created woman to be a help meet for man ("a helper to suit him" — Moffatt). Genesis 2:18. She was created to mother the people of the earth. Genesis 2:20; 23-24.

10. **WHAT WAS THE SITUATION THAT PRODUCED SIN?**

Adam and Eve were created innocent and perfect; God then placed them in the perfect environment of the Garden of Eden; they were subjected to an absolutely simple test and warned of the consequences of disobedience. Satan was given the opportunity to mislead the man and woman if he could. Genesis 2:15-17, 25.

11. **WHEN DID THEIR INNOCENCE END?**

The woman fell through vanity and pride, and man sinned deliberately. 1 Timothy 2:14; Genesis 3:1-7.

12. **WHAT ARE THE FOUR RESULTS OF THE ORIGINAL SIN?**

[1] The Serpent: cursed by God, lost its beauty and position. 3:14.
[2] The Woman: motherhood linked with sorrow; headship of man. 3:16.
[3] The Man; to live by physical toil; sentenced to death. 3:17-19.
[4] The Earth: cursed for man's sake. 3:17-19; Note Romans 8:19-22.

13. **DID GOD OFFER ANY HOPE TO MAN?**

God made a covenant with man to eventually bring forth a Saviour who would bring an end to the conditions of the curse. Genesis 3:15; 22:18; Romans 8:21.

LESSON 8 STUDY QUESTIONS BASED ON "THE CREATION OF MAN AND THE APPEARANCE OF SIN"

1. Which is the principal creature on earth?
2. Who was the first man?
3. Does the Bible teach that Adam was created 4,000 B.C.?
4. What was the image of God?
5. Does man still bear the image of God?
6. Is man a spirit being?
7. How many parts are there in a man?
8. How was woman created?
9. Why was woman created?
10. What was the situation that produced sin?
11. When did their innocence end?
12. What are the four results of the original sin?
13. Did God offer any hope to man?

PART III.
DISPENSATIONAL TRUTH

PART III. DISPENSATIONAL TRUTH

PART III. DISPENSATIONAL TRUTH

LESSON 1: INTRODUCING "GOD'S PLAN OF THE AGES"

A careful study of the prophetic Chart of the Ages (given on page 58) will be of the greatest help in gaining a proper understanding of the Bible. Bible chronology is a fascinating study and of the utmost importance. The student who knows the "when" and the "why" of the major happenings in the Bible sees God's Plan of Redemption as an exciting PANORAMA OF TRUTH. That is the main purpose for our including Part III in your catechism course. By the time the student finishes this third section of catechism, he should be able to locate chronologically the various important events and teachings of the entire Bible. Every TIME prophecy can be measured out on this chart.

1. HERE ARE SOME DEFINITIONS:
   TIME: "The period during which an action, process, etc., continues; measured or measurable duration." — Webster.

   CHRONOLOGY: The science which treats the measuring of time by regular divisions and which assigns to events their proper dates.

2. A DESCRIPTION OF THE CHART:
   The chart covers TIME from the dawn to sunset of history; it covers the subject of BIBLE CHRONOLOGY from beginning to end.

   On the horizontal line in the middle of the chart will be found seven small semicircles, which represent the SEVEN DAYS of God's Plan of Redemption. Each of these days is one thousand years long. 2 Peter 3:8; Psalms 90:4; 84:10. In this section of study we will examine the major happenings in each of these days. Especially, we are concerned to discover the great events that are yet to transpire in the SIXTH DAY — the time in which we now live!

   The three larger semicircles on the horizontal line of the chart, spanning two of the smaller, are the lines representing the THREE dispensations of time. They are each two thousand years in length, CO-EQUAL! This fact alone constitutes one of the outstanding evidences that God is the author of them. Hebrews 11:3 teaches that "worlds" ("ages" in the Greek) were framed by the Word of God; this also implies that the ages were measured by the Spirit of God, as we shall find later.

3. THE FIRST DISPENSATION is the dispensation of the FATHER GOD. It reaches from Adam to Abraham, a period of 2,000 years. God as the Father is the author of the first covenants, the first prophecies and the first promises: Genesis 3:15; 5:24; 6:18; 5:1-18. The outstanding personality of this dispensation (as concerns God's dealings with man) is that of God the Father whose name is "The LORD" or "Jehovah."

55

4.   THE CENTRAL DISPENSATION is that of the Son of God. It is bounded on one side by the covenants with Abraham (Genesis 15:1-18) which were sealed in the blood of circumcision and sacrifice, and on the other side by the shedding of the precious blood of Jesus Christ (Matthew 27:29-38; Hebrews 9:11-15). The MIDDLE dispensation is brought in by the offering of Isaac, the only begotten son of Abraham and Sarah, and reaches its end in the offering up of Jesus, the only begotten Son of God (Genesis 32:1-14; John 3:16). It is the dispensation of the central personality of the Godhead — Jesus the Son of God.

5.   THE LAST DISPENSATION is that of the Holy Ghost. It begins with the great outpouring of the Holy Spirit on the Day of Pentecost (Acts 2). The glorious climax of this age will take place shortly under the present outpouring of the Holy Spirit, in the perfection of the Church, the marriage of the Lamb, and the Second Coming of Jesus to earth (Epheaisns 5:25-27; Revelation 19:6-8; 1 Thessalonians 4:16).

6.   THESE DISPENSATIONS ARE A WITNESS of the operations of God in the salvation and redemption of mankind. 1 John 5:7, 8. At the top of the chart is the word "GOD," showing the absolute dominion of our God over all the periods of time from the beginning to the end. Under the word "God" will be noticed the Tri-unity of the Godhead as Father, Son and Holy Spirit — impressing upon the three dispensations the threefold nature of God; below that the combined personal Names of God for our day, "The Lord Jesus Christ." Also shown on the chart are the great signs of the heavens that blend their voices into the ages of time. The sun as the symbol of the Father; the moon as the symbol of the Son of God; and the stars as the symbol of the Holy Spirit.

7.   THE "RECEIVED CHRONOLOGY": The dates found in the margins of some study Bibles are not part of the inspired text of the Bible. About 1650 A.D., Archbishop Ussher worked out his interpretation of Bible chronology. He dates Adam at 4004 B.C., the Flood at 2348 B.C., Abraham's birth at 1996 B.C., the Exodus at 1491 B.C., and Solomon's Temple at 1012 B.C. It is very difficult to give exact dates, based on the chronological notices in the Bible. There is difference of opinion among Bible scholars, especially concerning the earlier dates. We have adopted the following general dates, and most Bible students are in approximate agreement: Adam's Sin, about 4000 B.C.; the Flood, about 2500 B.C.; Abraham, about 2000 B.C.; the Exodus, about 1500 B.C.; David, about 1000 B.C.; destruction of Jerusalem 586 B.C.

LESSON 1 STUDY QUESTIONS BASED ON
"INTRODUCING 'GOD'S PLAN OF THE AGES' "

1. Give the definitions of "Time" and "Chronology."
2. Make a simple line drawing of the chart.
3. Describe the First Dispensation.
4. Describe the Central Dispensation.
5. Describe the Last Dispensation.
6. To what do the three Dispensations bear witness.
7. What does the term "Received Chronology" refer to? You should be able to give the approximate dates for Adam, Noah, Abraham, Moses, David, and the destruction of Jerusalem. Use the chart as a memory aid!

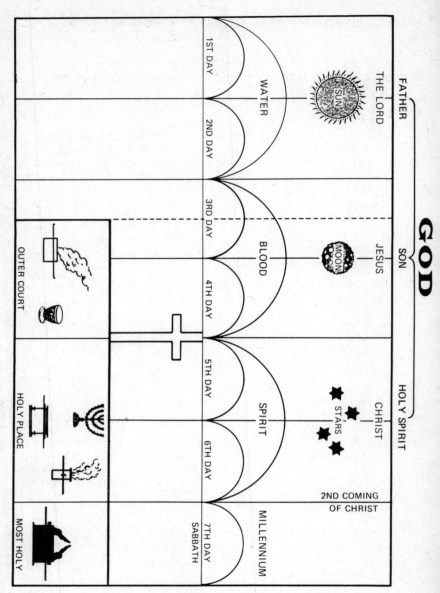

GOD

FATHER — THE LORD

1ST DAY · WATER · SUN

2ND DAY

SON — JESUS

3RD DAY · BLOOD · MOON

4TH DAY

OUTER COURT

HOLY SPIRIT — CHRIST

5TH DAY · SPIRIT · STARS

6TH DAY

HOLY PLACE

2ND COMING OF CHRIST

7TH DAY · SABBATH · MILLENNIUM

MOST HOLY

LESSON 2: MAJOR HAPPENINGS OF THE THREE DISPENSATIONS

1. HOW LONG IS THE FIRST DISPENSATION?
    2000 years, from Adam to Abraham.

2. WHAT ARE THE IMPORTANT BIBLE EVENTS DURING THIS TIME?
    Adam's sin, 4000 B.C.
    Enoch translated, 3000 B.C. (Genesis 5:24).
    Noah's ark and the flood, 2500 B.C. (Genesis 6 through 9).
    The tower of Babel and the confusion of languages (Genesis 11).

3. WHO WERE THE PATRIARCHS?
    This is the title that is given to those men of ancient times who walked with
    God and were the head of their families. Generally, the men who lived
    during this first dispensation were called patriarchs.

4. HOW DOES GOD REVEAL HIMSELF DURING THE FIRST DISPENSATION?
    We see God the Father revealed during the first dispensation.

5. WHAT IS THE KEY THOUGHT OF THE FIRST DISPENSATION?
    The flood of water to judge the sin of the earth. This is an illustration of
    the Christian's water baptism.

6. HOW LONG IS THE SECOND DISPENSATION?
    2000 years, from Abraham to Jesus' crucifixion.

7. WHAT ARE THE IMPORTANT BIBLE EVENTS DURING THIS TIME?
    God's covenant with Abraham, Isaac and Jacob (Genesis), 2000 B.C.
    The Exodus, Moses and the 10 Commandments (Exodus), 1500 B.C.
    The Period of the Judges (Judges).
    The Period of the Kings and Prophets, beginning with Saul (1 Samuel).
    David, Solomon and building the Temple, approximately 1000 B.C.
    The Division of David's Kingdom (Kings and Chronicles).
    Captivity and Restoration of the Jews (Ezra, Esther and Nehemiah).

8. WHAT IS THE KEY THOUGHT OF THE SECOND DISPENSATION?
    From Abraham to Christ we find the SHEDDING OF BLOOD commanded.
    Both in the circumcision of every male Israelite and in the animal sacrifices
    whose blood brought atonement, we find that the key thought is blood
    sacrifice. This is an illustration of the Christian's salvation experience
    through the blood of Christ. Hebrews 9:11-15 .

9. WHAT PERSONALITY OF THE GODHEAD IS REVEALED IN THE SECOND
    DISPENSATION?
    The Lord Jesus Christ is shown prophetically throughout this time of
    blood sacrifice.

10. HOW LONG IS THE THIRD DISPENSATION?
    2000 years, from Jesus' crucifixion to His second coming.

11. WHAT ARE THE IMPORTANT BIBLE EVENTS DURING THIS TIME?
    This dispensation is the "Church Age."
    The history of the early Apostolic Church is given in The Acts.
    The spiritual decline of the Church as given in Church History.
    The "Dark Ages" of about 1000 A.D.
    The restoration of the Church as great truths broke upon the Church.
    The final last day outpouring of the Holy Spirit.

12. WHAT PERSONALITY OF THE GODHEAD DOMINATES THIS THIRD DISPENSATION?
    This is the age of the Holy Spirit. 2 Corinthians 5:16; Ephesians 2:18.

13. WHAT IS THE KEY THOUGHT OF THE THIRD DISPENSATION?
    This entire era is the story of the activity of the Holy Spirit in the life of the Church. It illustrates graphically the need of every believer to receive "The Baptism with the Holy Ghost."

14. THE SIGNIFICANCE OF THE THREE DISPENSATIONS.
    The number THREE is the signature of God. We see it everywhere. Look at the construction of plants or at your own body. God does things frequently in three's. We have shown that the personality of God as Father, Son and Holy Spirit is revealed in the three major dispensations. Also, we see the three basic experiences of every Christian — Salvation through the Blood, Baptism in Water and the Baptism with the Holy Spirit. These thoughts show the significance of John's statement in 1 John 5:7 and 8!

LESSON 2 STUDY QUESTIONS BASED ON
"MAJOR HAPPENINGS OF THE THREE DISPENSATIONS"

1. How long is the first dispensation?
2. What are the important Bible events during this time?
3. Who were the Patriarchs?
4. How does God reveal himself during the first dispensation?
5. What is the key thought of the first dispensation?
6. How long is the second dispensation?
7. What are the important Bible events during this time?
8. What is the key thought of the second dispensation?
9. What personality of the Godhead is revealed in the second dispenation?
10. How long is the third dispensation?
11. What are the important Bible events during this time?
12. What personality of the Godhead dominates this third dispensation?
13. Explain the significance of the three dispensations and 1 John 5:7 and 8.

LESSON 3: PROPHETIC PROOFS OF GOD'S PLAN

NOTE: THE PURPOSE OF THIS LESSON is to give Scriptural proofs that God's Plan is actually a "Week of Redemption" composed of seven days, each of which is equal to 1,000 years. It may appear at first that the unusual collection of illustrations given below is a poor example of Bible exegesis. We believe, however, that prayerful reflection on these thoughts will convince the student that God Himself has inspired these Bible pictures to help us better retain the Truth.

1. ONE DAY OF THE LORD = 1,000 YEARS.
    2 Peter 3:8; Psalms 84:10; 90:4.

2. THE PASSOVER LAMB WAS TO BE HIDDEN FOUR DAYS.
    Exodus 12:3-6. For four days (or, 4,000 years) from Adam to the Cross, Jesus was "kept," destined to die as the final Passover Lamb for the sins of the world. 1 Peter 1:20; Revelation 13:8.

3. THE "PASSION WEEK" ILLUSTRATES GOD'S WEEK.
    The Passion Week recorded in the Gospels is actually a small replica of the more extended plan of the ages. Daniel 9:27 states that the Christ was to cause sacrifice to cease "in the midst of the week" — which, of course, means Wednesday, not "Good Friday." Note "three days" in Matthew 12:40. Thus, Jesus fulfilled His redemptive ministry on earth at the close of the fourth day, both in God's Week as well as the Passion Week.

4. THE "MILLENNIUM" WILL BE GOD'S SABBATH.
    The word "millennium" does not occur in the Bible; however, since it is an English word meaning "a thousand years" (Webster), it is perfectly proper to use it. The expression "thousand years," occurs six times in Revelation 20:2, 3, 4, 5, 6, 7; the context indicates that this is the seventh 1,000 year day (or, Sabbath) of God's Plan of the Ages.

5. PETER USES THE EXPRESSION "IN THE LAST DAYS."
    Acts 2:17. Since some of what Peter mentioned has not yet come to pass, how could it be the LAST days? Answer: Peter lived in the fifth day of God's Plan and the Church today lives in the sixth day; hence, both the early Church and today's Church live in the "last days."

6. HOSEA MADE AN UNUSUAL PROPHECY.
    Hosea 6:2. "After two days" refers to the 2,000 years of Gospel Age, while "third day" refers to the seventh day or Millennium. The First Resurrection occurs at the end of the 2,000 year Gospel Age.

7. A SIGNIFICANT THOUGHT ABOUT GATHERING MANNA.
    Exodus 16:11-35. "Manna" was the bread that God supplied Israel for their daily food ration; however, on the SIXTH DAY they were to gather a

DOUBLE PORTION to carry them through the Sabbath. This is a prophetic picture of God's special outpouring and work in our hearts in the last of the Gospel Age to carry us on into the Millennium.

8. **EZEKIEL'S MEASUREMENTS HAVE PROPHETIC IMPORT.**
Ezekiel 47:1-12. The four 1,000 cubital measurements of the Angel of the Lord reach from Abraham (2000 B.C.) to the Second Coming of Christ (2000 A.D.); the measurements cover four prophetic days in God's plan.

9. **THE ARK OF THE COVENANT WAS REMOVED FROM THE PEOPLE.**
Joshua 3:4. The 2,000 cubits between the Ark and the people is a prophetic measurement of the 2,000 years of the Gospel Age that separates Israel under the Law from the full Glory of God during the Millennium.

10. **THE MEASUREMENTS OF THE TABERNACLE ARE PROPHETIC.**
Outer Court Curtain: 300 x 5 = 1500 sq. cu.; 1500 years of Law.
Holy Place: 10 x 10 x 20 = 2000 cu. cubits; 2000 years of the Gospel.
Most Holy: 10 x 10 x 10 = 1000 cu. cubits; 1000 years of Millennium.

11. **THE BRASEN SEA OF SOLOMON'S TEMPLE IS A GRAPHIC PICTURE.**
1 Kings 7:26; 2 Chronicles 4:5. This great brass basin rested on the backs of twelve oxen. Holding 2,000 baths in regular use and 3,000 baths when brim full, this "sea" is a type of the Gospel Age of 2,000.

12. **WE'RE GOING TO HAVE A JUBILEE!**
Leviticus 25 and 27. The Jubilee = 50 years; 120 Jubilees = 6,000 years. Each Dispensation of time measures 40 Jubilees or 2,000 years. Three Dispensations of 40 Jubilees = 120 Jubilees. Jesus will come in the 120th Jubilee.

13. **THE DESTRUCTION OF THE 2,000 SWINE IS SYMBOLIC.**
Mark 5:13; Revelation 12:9. The destruction of the 2,000 swine is prophetic of the casting down, binding, and sealing in the abyss of the Devil at the end of the present dispensation of 2,000 years.

14. **ANALYZE THE WEEK OF CREATION IN GENESIS.**
Genesis 1. The events of the seven days of creation find remarkable spiritual application in the seven 1,000 year days of God's Plan.

LESSON 3 STUDY QUESTIONS BASED ON "PROPHETIC PROOFS OF GOD'S PLAN"

1. One day of the Lord is equal to how many years?
2. How many days was the Passover Lamb to be hidden?
3. In what way is the Passion Week like God's Week?

LESSION 3 STUDY QUESTIONS BASED ON
"PROPHETIC PROOFS OF GOD'S PLAN" (Continued)

4. Is it Biblically accurate to refer to a Millennium?
5. What does Peter mean by "in the last days"?
6. How does Hosea's unusual prophecy apply to the Church Age?
7. What significance would gathering manna on the sixth day have for us?
8. What is the prophetic meaning of Ezekiel's measurements?
9. How far was the Ark of the Covenant removed from the people? Why?
10. Explain the prophetic time measurements in the Tabernacle.
11. What does the brasen sea in Solomon's Temple picture for us?
12. In which Jubilee will Jesus come back to earth?
13. The destruction of the 2,000 swine symbolizes what event?
14. What parallels can you draw between the week of creation in Genesis and God's Plan of the Ages?

A FINAL SUGGESTION ON
PART III. DISPENSATIONAL TRUTH

Each student of this catechism should be able to draw "God's Plan of the Ages" from memory. It should become so deeply imbedded in your thinking that you will automatically place any character of the Bible in his proper chronological position. It is our considered opinion that of all the charts and plans available, this simple straightforward approach is the best. It has been used effectively in teaching Juniors in Sunday School as well as mature adults. Use it and you will see its greatness in the presentation of the panorama of the Scriptures.

THE SEVEN COVENANTS OF GOD

PART IV. THE SEVEN COVENANTS OF GOD

PART IV. THE 7 COVENANTS OF GOD

LESSON 1: INTRODUCTION TO THE COVENANTS

1. **WHAT IS A COVENANT?**

    A covenant is a contract or agreement drawn up between two parties. As we will use the term, "covenant" refers to the binding agreements drawn up between God and His people.

2. **IS A COVENANT AND A TESTAMENT THE SAME THING?**

    In the Bible, the term "testament" refers to a covenant.

3. **WHAT IS THE OLD TESTAMENT OR COVENANT?**

    When someone refers to the "Old Testament," generally they mean the first thirty-nine books of the Bible, from Genesis through Malachi. Actually, during the 4,000 years of the Old Testament period, God made a number of covenants with men. We have chosen six of the great covenants of the Old Testament period for our study. Strictly speaking, the Old Covenant or Testament is the SUM TOTAL of all the covenants made during the period from Adam to Christ.

4. **WHAT IS THE NEW TESTAMENT?**

    When the Lord Jesus Christ died on the cross, He brought in a New Covenant agreement between God and man. This NEW Testament fulfills, absorbs and supercedes all of God's previous agreements with mankind. This New Testament is described in the last twenty-seven books of the Bible. Hebrews 8:6-13; Jeremiah 31:31-34.

5. **HOW DOES THE BIBLE ILLUSTRATE THE OLD COVENANT?**

    The Old Covenant is likened unto the law of marriage, which can only be dissolved by death or unfaithfulness. Romans 7:1-4; Jeremiah 3; Isaiah 54; Galatians 4:26-28.

6. **HOW DOES THE BIBLE ILLUSTRATE THE NEW COVENANT?**

    In two ways:

    [1] The New Covenant is the new marriage; Jesus Christ is the bridegroom and the Church is the bride. The Old Covenant relationship between God and His people died with Christ on the cross; now, God's people are free to be joined to a new husband and covenant.

    [2] The Bible likens the New Covenant to an inheritance will or testament. Just as a will goes into effect when the maker (or, testator) dies, so the New Covenant or will went into effect when Christ the maker died. Hebrews 9:16, 17.

7. **WHY DOES GOD MAKE COVENANTS?**

    God makes covenants with man to illustrate two important points:

[1] God's Word is absolutely reliable.

[2] Man's word is absolutely unreliable.

Read: Numbers 23:19; Isaiah 14:24; 40:5; 45:23; 2 Samuel 15:29; Malachi 3:6; 2 Corinthians 7:10; Romans 11:29; Titus 1:2; James 1:17; Hebrews 6:13-18.

8. WHAT PURPOSE IS FULFILLED WHEN WE KNOW MAN'S UNRELIABILITY? When a person really understands man's failure and God's success, he can rightly appreciate that [1] God's grace HAS SAVED him, and [2] God's grace at work IS SAVING him, and [3] God's grace ultimately WILL FINISH salvation in him. Hebrews 4:16, Ephesians 2:8, 9.

9. WHAT ARE THE SEVEN MAJOR COVENANTS OF THE BIBLE?

[1] The Edenic Covenant — Adam before sin.

[2] The Adamic Covenant — Adam after sin.

[3] The Noahic Covenant — Noah and the rainbow.

[4] The Abrahamic Covenant — Abraham and circumcision.

[5] The Mosaic Covenant — Moses and the Law.

[6] The Davidic Covenant — David and his Throne.

[7] THE NEW COVENANT OF OUR LORD JESUS CHRIST.

NOTE: This part of the catechism will deal with just the first six covenants. The entire remaining parts and lessons will be an elaboration of the NEW COVENANT, which is our inheritance today.

LESSON 1 STUDY QUESTIONS BASED ON
"INTRODUCTION TO THE COVENANTS"

1. What is a covenant?

2. Is a covenant and a testament the same thing?

3. What is the Old Testament or Covenant?

4. What is the New Testament?

5. How does the Bible illustrate the Old Covenant?

6. How does the Bible illustrate the New Covenant?

7. Why does God make covenants?

8. What purpose is fulfilled when we know man's unreliability?

9. What are the seven major covenants of the Bible?

LESSON 2:   THE EDENIC COVENANT (ADAM IN THE GARDEN OF EDEN)

1.   WHAT WAS THE EDENIC COVENANT?

The Edenic Covenant was the agreement and relationship that existed between God and Adam in the Garden of Eden before Adam sinned.

2.   WHAT WERE THINGS LIKE UNDER THE EDENIC COVENANT? Genesis 1 and 2.

[1]   Man bore the image of God (1:26), and had unashamed fellowship with God (note 3:8-11).
[2]   Man had dominion over all God's creation. 1:26; 2:15; Psalms 8.
[3]   Man was fruitful and productive. 1:28.
[4]   Man was innocent of lust (2:25), and had but one wife (Matthew 19:8).
[5]   Man had creative genius. 2:19, 20.
[6]   Man was a vegetarian (no blood was shed to provide food). 1:29.
[7]   Man lived and worked in a garden prepared for him by God (2:8), and used the 7th day of each week as a Sabbath (2:2).

3.   WHAT DID GOD REQUIRE OF ADAM AND EVE IN THIS COVENANT?

God's covenant with Adam required him to be productive (1:28), subdue and dominate the creation (1:28), dress and keep the Garden of Eden (2:15), and ABSTAIN from the tree of the knowledge of good and evil (2:17).

4.   WHAT (IN SIMPLE TERMS) DID ADAM DO WHEN HE SINNED?

To put it simply, Adam's sin was being disobedient to God's Word. Man transferred the control of his life from God to himself.

5.   WHY DID GOD MAKE MAN SO THAT HE COULD SIN?

Well, is there any other way He could have made him, except as a machine, a puppet, or an animal guided only by instinct? Could there be a moral creature without the power to choose? FREEDOM is God's gift to man — freedom to think, freedom to choose, freedom of conscience — even though man uses his freedom to reject and disobey God.

6.   DID GOD FOREKNOW THAT MAN WOULD SIN?

Yes, and He foreknew the fearful consequences, but He also foreknew the ultimate outcome.

7.   WHAT WAS THE GREAT PURPOSE THAT GOD HAD IN MIND?

God's greatest desire is to bless man with a nobility of character like His own. This desired perfection in man, however, must be a result of man's will as well as God's creation. The Garden of Eden was basically a simple test of character and will, set amid every conceivable blessing. Man learned in no uncertain terms that character failure would bring death. Genesis 2:17; Ezekiel 18:4, 20. Now, God's program is to develop within fallen man a

69

desire and will to OVERCOME in spite of the testings of sin and Satan. Revelation 12:11; 21:7.

8. HOW DID THE SERPENT BEGUILE THE WOMAN?

Note: 2 Corinthians 11:3, 14; Revelation 12:9; 20:2.

[1] Questioning the Word. 3:1.   [4] Adulterating the Word. 2:17.
[2] Adding to the Word. 3:2, 3.   [5] Lying against the Word. 3:4.
[3] Subtracting from the Word. 2:16.   [6] Slandering the Word. 3:5.

9. WHAT ARE THE THREE LUSTS THAT THE SERPENT EVOKED IN EVE?

1 John 2:16; Genesis 3:6.

[1] LUST of the flesh: ". . . saw that the tree was good for food . . . ."
[2] LUST of the eyes: ". . . it was pleasant to the eyes . . . ."
[3] The PRIDE of life: ". . . to be desired to make one wise . . . ."

NOTE: Jesus conquered these lusts in the Wilderness. Luke 4:1-13.

10. HOW IS A SIN COMMITTED?

The following formula is given in James 1:12-15:

PERSONAL LUST + ENTICEMENT + SIN = DEATH
(sinful desire)   (tempted with   (act of
                        evil)   lust)

Note also Romans 7:5 and Galatians 5:24.

11. THE RESULTS OF ADAM'S DISOBEDIENCE and the broken covenant will be analyzed in the next lesson, since it is the covenant that was based on the broken Edenic Covenant.

LESSON 2 STUDY QUESTIONS BASED ON "THE EDENIC COVENANT"

1. What was the Edenic Covenant?
2. What were things like under the Edenic Covenant?
3. What did God require of Adam and Eve in this Covenant?
4. What (in simple terms) did Adam do when he sinned?
5. Why did God make man so that he could sin?
6. Did not God foreknow that man would sin?
7. What was the great purpose that God had in mind?
8. How did the Serpent beguile the woman?
9. What are the three lusts that the Serpent evoked in Eve?
10. How is a sin committed?

LESSON 3: THE ADAMIC COVENANT (ADAM DRIVEN FROM THE GARDEN)

1. **DOES GOD EVER BREAK A COVENANT WITH MAN?**
    God never breaks a covenant. When man has once violated a covenant with God, however, a new relationship exists and God acts accordingly. 1 Kings 8:23; Deuteronomy 7:9; Nehemiah 1:5; 9:32-38; Daniel 9:4.

2. **WHEN DID THE EDENIC COVENANT END?**
    The benefits of the Edenic Covenant were lost to man when Eve fell through deception and Adam sinned deliberately. Genesis 3:1-7; 1 Timothy 2:14.

3. **WHAT WAS THE ADAMIC COVENANT?**
    When man sinned, he stood before God as a law-breaker, and as such subject to the justice of God. The Adamic Covenant is God's statement of both justice and mercy for Adam's disobedience.

4. **WHAT WERE THE PHYSICAL CONSEQUENCES OF ADAM'S DISOBEDIENCE?**
    [1] The SERPENT: cursed by God, lost its beauty and position. 3:14.
    [2] The WOMAN: motherhood linked with sorrow; to be under the headship of man. 3:16.
    [3] The MAN: to live by physical toil; sentenced to death. 3:17-19.
    [4] The EARTH: cursed for man's sake. 3:17-19; Note Romans 8:19-22.

5. **WHAT WERE THE SPIRITUAL CONSEQUENCES OF THE BROKEN COVENANT?**
    [1] Man was fearful in God's presence. Genesis 3:10.
    [2] Man died spiritually when he broke the covenant, and began dying physically as well. Genesis 2:17; 3:19, 22; 5:3, 4. Note that he lived just short of a Lord's day — 930 years.
    [3] Man was driven from the Paradise of God. 3:22-24.

6. **WAS THERE ANY SALVATION FOR ADAM AND EVE?**
    Although the wages of Adam's sin was death (Romans 6:23), God did extend mercy. In Genesis 3:21, we find the record of the first vicarious sacrifice. The coats of skins which God made for Adam and Eve had necessitated FOR THE FIRST TIME the death of an animal. This, of course, is a beautiful type of Christ dying for us to provide us with a covering for our sin. Note how Adam's act and Christ's act affect us today. Romans 5:12-19.

7. **IS THERE ANY PROMISE OF FUTURE REDEMPTION?**
    Thank God for the promised Redeemer, mentioned in Genesis 3:15, Jesus Christ is the promised Seed that will bring victory.

8. **THE BRUISING OF THE SERPENT'S HEAD IS A REMARKABLE TRUTH:**
    Genesis 3:15; Joshua 10:24; Judges 4:21; (5:26); 9:53; Psalms 68:21;

71

Isaiah 28:21; Habakkuk 3:13; Romans 16:20; Mark 16:18; Revelation 12:9; 20:10.

9.   DOES THE BIBLE EVER MENTION THE TREE OF LIFE AGAIN?
Read Revelation 2:7 and 22:2.

LESSON 3 STUDY QUESTIONS BASED ON
"THE ADAMIC COVENANT"

1.   Does God ever break a covenant with man?
2.   When did the Edenic Covenant end?
3.   What was the Adamic Covenant?
4.   What were the physical consequences of Adam's disobedience?
5.   What were the spiritual consequences of the broken covenant?
6.   Was there any salvation for Adam and Eve?
7.   Is there any promise of future redemption?
8.   The bruising of the Serpent's head is a remarkable truth. Can you give any other references about this theme?
9.   Does the Bible ever mention the Tree of Life again?

LESSON 4: THE NOAHIC COVENANT (NOAH AND THE RAINBOW)

1. WHAT WAS THE HISTORICAL SETTING FOR THE NOAHIC COVENANT?
   "The wickedness of man was great in the earth and every imagination of the thoughts of his heart was only evil continually." Genesis 6:5.
   "The earth was filled with violence." Genesis 6:11.
   "All flesh had corrupted his way upon the earth." Genesis 6:12.

2. HOW DID GOD FEEL ABOUT THIS SITUATION?
   God "regretted" that He had made man and it grieved Him. Genesis 6:6.
   God said, "I will destroy them with the earth." Genesis 6:13.

3. DOES THE WORLD SITUATION OF THAT TIME HAVE A MESSAGE FOR OUR DAY?
   Yes! Jesus clearly taught that the days immediately preceding His Second Coming would be like those violent days that preceded the flood. Matthew 24:37-39.

4. WHO WAS NOAH?
   Noah was a descendant of Adam through Seth who lived about 2500 B.C.
   He was destined to greatness by prophecy. Genesis 5:28, 29.

5. WHAT WAS THE NOAHIC COVENANT?
   Although God was angry at the violence of mankind, He made covenant with Noah. Noah was told to build a large ark (boat) which would be used by God for the preservation of Noah's family and members of the animal kingdom. The world would be repopulated by these survivors.

6. WHAT KIND OF A MAN WAS NOAH?
   [1] Noah was "favored" of the Lord. Genesis 6:8.
   [2] He was a just man, and
   [3] Perfect in his generations. 6:9.
   [4] Noah walked with God. 6:9.
   [5] Noah was obedient to God's Word. 6:22.
   [6] Noah was a worshipper. 8:20.
   [7] He was a "preacher of righteousness." 2 Peter 2:5.

7. WHY WAS NOAH ESTEEMED RIGHTEOUS BEFORE GOD?
   The obedience of Noah's faith yielded righteousness. Romans 4:22; Hebrews 11:7; Genesis 7:1.

8. WHAT WAS THE SIZE OF NOAH'S ARK?
   "Considering that a cubit is 25 inches, the ark was about 625 ft. long, 104 ft. wide, and 62-1/2 ft. high. Up to 1850 A.D. there was no ship in the history of the world as large as the ark. Of the world's steamships up to 1932 less than one percent were as large; and only 160 were longer, seven wider and eight higher than the ark. Only six had a greater tonnage. The capacity of the ark was equivalent in tonnage to more than 600 freight cars,

which would form a train about four miles long capable of handling over 90,000,000 pounds.

The ark was easily big enough for all it was to hold. The fish and other sea creatures stayed in the sea; insects were small as well as snakes and lizards. The average size of most mammals was no larger than a dog. The birds could have easily lodged in the ceilings or been hung up in cages. An ox is allowed 20 sq. ft. on a modern vessel. If this much room was allowed in the ark for each of the larger mammals, there would have been ample room for all including food for a year and 17 days."

— Dake's Annotated Reference Bible

9. HOW DID GOD DESTROY THE WICKED PEOPLE OF NOAH'S DAY?
God destroyed the wicked with a tremendous flood of water. Genesis 7:11, 19, 21, 22.

10. HOW MUCH TIME WAS ACTUALLY SPENT IN THE ARK?
By comparing the following references, you will discover that Noah was actually on the ark 1 YEAR AND 17 DAYS, 5 months floating, 7 months on the mountain. Genesis 7:4, 10, 11, 12, 24; 8:3-5, 13, 14-19.

11. WHAT WAS NOAH'S FIRST ACT IN THE NEW WORLD?
Noah worshipped God. Genesis 8:20.

12. WHAT WAS INCLUDED IN THE NOAHIC COVENANT?
[1] God would never destroy the earth again by flood. 8:21; 9:11.
[2] The earth would always have its seasonal changes. 8:22.
[3] Noah's sons were to multiply and replenish the earth. 9:1, 7.
[4] The eating of meat was permitted (but not blood). 9:3.
[5] God warned against shedding man's blood. 9:5, 6.

13. WE STILL HAVE THE SIGN OF THE NOAHIC COVENANT WITH US!
God gave mankind the rainbow as a "token" of his covenant. 9:12.

14. THE NEXT TIME THE WORLD IS DESTROYED, HOW WILL IT BE DONE?
The world will be destroyed by fire. Note 2 Peter 3: 5-13.

15. WHAT TWO THINGS DID NOAH DO THAT MUST BE DONE BY THE CHURCH?
Noah preached and Noah builded. 2 Peter 2:5 calls him a "preacher of righteousness." It is a significant truth that while he preached, he was careful to secure his own destiny through the boat!

LESSON 4 STUDY QUESTIONS BASED ON
"THE NOAHIC COVENANT"

1. What was the historical setting for the Noahic Covenant?
2. How did God feel about this situation?
3. Does the world situation of that time have a message for our day?
4. Who was Noah?
5. What was the Noahic Covenant?
6. What kind of a man was Noah?
7. Why was Noah esteemed righteous before God?
8. What was the size of Noah's ark?
9. How did God destroy the wicked people of Noah's day?
10. How much time was actually spent on the ark?
11. What was Noah's first act in the new world?
12. What was included in the Noahic Covenant?
13. Do we still have the sign of the Noahic Covenant with us?
14. The next time the world is destroyed, how will it be done?
15. What two things did Noah do that must be done by the Church?

LESSON 5: THE ABRAHAMIC COVENANT (ABRAHAM AND CIRCUMCISION)

1. WHY IS ABRAHAM SUCH AN IMPORTANT FIGURE IN BIBLE HISTORY?
   Abraham is the man that God chose to produce the nation that would in turn produce the Christ.

2. DID ABRAHAM HAVE MUCH ENCOURAGEMENT TO BELIEVE IN GOD?
   No. Abraham's own father was an idolator (Joshua 24:2). His countrymen were idolators. Ur was in Babylonia, where there were all types of idolatrous worship.

3. HOW DID ABRAHAM COME TO KNOW THE TRUE GOD?
   No doubt, by Divine revelation. Genesis 12:1; Acts 7:3; Hebrews 11:8. Also, since Noah's life extended to the birth of Abraham, it is possible that Abraham could have heard about the flood from Shem (Noah's son), and also Methuselah's account of Adam and Eve in Eden!

4. WHAT WAS THE CHIEF CHARACTERISTIC OF ABRAHAM?
   Abraham was a man of faith. Romans 4:20, 21; Hebrews 11:8-19. This means that Abraham believed that God would do what He said He would do. He learned to put his confidence in what God said.

5. WHAT IS UNIQUE ABOUT THE ABRAHAMIC COVENANT?
   The Abrahamic Covenant was progressively revealed to Abraham, rather than given all at once. Genesis 12 through 22.

6. HOW MANY TIMES DID GOD SPEAK WITH ABRAHAM?
   According to the record, God came to Abraham SEVEN times. Genesis 12:1, 7; 13:14; 15:1; 17:1; 18:1; 22.

7. IN SIMPLEST TERMS, WHAT DOES THE ABRAHAMIC COVENANT INVOLVE?
   On page 78 you will find fourteen great promises of the Abrahamic Covenant that were progressively revealed; but in simplest terms, this Covenant involved:
   [1] The Promised Land,   [2] The Promised People,
   [3] The Promised Seed,   [4] The Promised Blessing for all nations.

8. WHAT IS THE KEY CHAPTER IN THIS STUDY OF THIS COVENANT?
   Of the many chapters which describe the life of Abraham, Genesis 17 goes to the very heart of the Covenant. In this chapter the word "covenant" appears 13 times.

9. TWO SIGNIFICANT THINGS HAPPENED TO ABRAHAM IN THIS CHAPTER:
   [1] His name was changed, and
   [2] He was circumcised.

10. WHY DID GOD CHANGE HIS NAME?
    "Abram" means "exalted Father" and "Abraham" means "Father of a great

multitude." Thus, Abram ceased to be exalted, but from this crushing of self came the spiritual potential of blessing the nations. This is the same principle mentioned in John 12:24.

11. WHY DID GOD PLACE SUCH AN IMPORTANCE ON CIRCUMCISION?

In Genesis 17:11, circumcision is called a "token of the covenant." This means that it was the seal or pledge of the agreement between Abraham's descendents and God. Every family of Israel would thereby have a tangible sign in their leader of God's covenant relationship. Also, it indicated that this was a fleshly covenant, and was a prophetic sign or picture of that which God wanted to accomplish in the human heart through the New Covenant. Colossians 2:11, 12.

12. SHOULD CHILDREN BE CIRCUMCISED TODAY?

Today there is no SPIRITUAL benefit in physical circumcision. Galatians 5:6. There is, of course, a physical benefit. Please note the interesting chapter on this subject in the book, "None of These Diseases" by Dr. S. I. McMillen.

13. WHAT WAS ABRAHAM'S GREAT FAILURE?

Abraham tried to accomplish the impossible through his own strength. He found, however, that God would not bless the child of the flesh with the Covenant — this was reserved for the miracle child of promise. Genesis 16.

LESSON 5 STUDY QUESTIONS BASED ON "THE ABRAHAMIC COVENANT"

1. Why is Abraham such an important figure in Bible history?
2. Did Abraham have much encouragement to believe in God?
3. How did Abraham come to know the true God?
4. What was the chief characteristic of Abraham?
5. What is unique about the Abrahamic Covenant?
6. How many times did God speak with Abraham?
7. In simplest terms, what does the Abrahamic Covenant involve?
8. What is the key chapter in the study of this covenant?
9. What two significant things happened to Abraham in Genesis 17?
10. Why did God change his name?
11. Why did God place such an importance on circumcision?
12. Should children be circumcised today?
13. What was Abraham's greatest failure?

APPENDIX TO LESSON 5: THE ABRAHAMIC COVENANT

The Fourteen Great Promises of God to Abraham (Genesis 12 through 22):

1. "MAKE OF THEE A GREAT NATION"
   12:2; 18:18; 46:3, 4.

2. "I WILL BLESS THEE"
   12:2; 14:19; 22:17.

3. "MAKE THY NAME GREAT"
   12:2.

4. "THOU SHALT BE A BLESSING"
   12:2.

5. "I WILL BLESS THEM THAT BLESS THEE"
   12:3; 27:29; Numbers 24:9.

6. "CURSE HIM THAT CURSETH THEE"
   12:3; 27:29; Numbers 24:9.

7. "IN THEE SHALL ALL FAMILIES OF THE EARTH BE BLESSED"
   12:3; 18:18.

8. "UNTO THY SEED WILL I GIVE THIS LAND"
   12:7; 13:14, 15, 17; 15:7, 8; 17:8; 24:7; 26:4.

9. "I WILL MAKE THY SEED AS THE DUST OF THE EARTH"
   13:16; 15:5; 22:17.

10. "A FATHER OF MANY NATIONS"
    17:4.

11. " WILL MAKE NATIONS OF THEE"
    17:6.

12. "KINGS SHALL COME OF THEE"
    17:6, 16.

13. "IN ISAAC SHALL THY SEED BE CALLED"
    21:12.

14. "THY SEED SHALL POSSESS THE GATE OF HIS ENEMIES"
    22:17.

LESSON 6: THE MOSAIC COVENANT (MOSES AND THE LAW)

INTRODUCTION:

The story of Moses is long and exciting. The covenant which God made with Moses on Mt. Sinai is what we refer to as the Mosaic Covenant. Actually, Moses received three things on the mountain: The Ten Commandments (or the Moral Law), the Levitical Laws, and the Blueprint of the tabernacle. This study will cover only the Ten Commandments.

1. WHAT ARE THE TEN COMMANDMENTS?

The Ten Commandments are the basis of the Moral Law of God. Exodus 20:3-17. The Lord gave the Ten Commandments, but He did not say which is the First, the Second, etc. Not all churches use the same order in numbering the Commandments.

2. HOW DID GOD GIVE THE LAW?

Originally, God wrote the Law into the heart of man. For Israel, God arranged the Law in Ten Commandments — written on two tables of stone — and proclaimed it through Moses. Exodus 20; Romans 2:14, 15.

3. THE FIRST TABLE OF THE LAW HAD TO DO WITH OUR DUTY TO GOD

It may be summarized by Matthew 22:37, "Thou shalt love the Lord thy God with all thy heart, and with all thy soul, and with all thy mind."

4. THE SECOND TABLE OF THE LAW HAD TO DO WITH OUR DUTY TO MAN

It may be summarized by Matthew 22:39, "Thou shalt love thy neighbor as thyself."

5. WHAT IS THE SUMMARY OF ALL THE COMMANDMENTS?

Love is the summary of all the commandments.
"Love is the fulfilling of the Law." Romans 13:10.

6. TO WHOM DOES GOD REFER WHEN HE SAYS "THOU SHALT" IN THE TEN COMMANDMENTS?

"Thou shalt" is God's direct command to me and all other human beings.

THE FIRST TABLE OF THE LAW, COMMANDMENTS 1 THROUGH 4

7. WHAT IS THE FIRST COMMANDMENT?

"Thou shalt have no other gods before me." Exodus 20:3.

8. WHAT DOES GOD REQUIRE OF US IN THE FIRST COMMANDMENT?

God requires that we fear, love and trust in Him above all things. The true God is to be the only object of our worship, prayer and religious activity. Psalms 33:8; Genesis 17:1; Proverbs 8:13; Matthew 22:37; Psalms 118:8; Proverbs 3:7. Note Daniel 3 and 2 Samuel 17.

9. WHAT DOES GOD FORBID IN THE FIRST COMMANDMENT?

God forbids us to have other gods instead of Him or in addition to Him;

in other words, He forbids idolatry. Matthew 4:10; Isaiah 42:8.

10. WHEN DO MEN HAVE OTHER GODS?

[1] When they regard and worship any creature as God. Psalms 115:3, 4; Exodus 32; 1 Kings 12:28; 18:18-29; Judges 16:23, 24.

[2] When they believe in a god that does not identify with and glorify the Lord Jesus Christ. 1 John 2:22; 23: 4:2; John 5:23; 17:3.

[3] When they fear, love or trust in any person or thing as they should fear, love and trust in God alone. Matthew 10:28, 37; Proverbs 3:5; Ephesians 5:5; Philippians 3:19.

11. IS JESUS CHRIST ANOTHER GOD?

No! Jesus is the Son of God; that is, He is God manifested in a physical, tangible way so that we might better understand God. John 1:1; 10:30; 14:7-11; 17:11; Matthew 1:23; 1 Timothy 3:16; 1 John 1:1, 2.

12. THE LORD JESUS CHRIST IS THE FULFILLMENT OF THE FIRST COMMANDMENT!

Read Hebrews 1. There you will find an array of statements proving that Jesus is Divine and worthy of all things due God. For instance, He is to be worshipped (v. 6); He is addressed as "God" (v. 8); He is acknowledged as the creator of all things (v. 2).

13. WHAT IS THE SECOND COMMANDMENT?

"Thou shalt not make unto thee any graven image." Exodus 20:4.

14. WHAT DOES THIS MEAN?

We are not to use any earthly material (earth, clay, metal, wood, stone or paint) to construct a figure that represents God. This refers to anything that can be seen, described or imagined as being Divine.

15. WHY DOES GOD FORBID IDOLATRY IN ANY FORM OR FASHION?

The God of the Bible is a jealous God and His glory and His praise He will not share with another. Exodus 20:5; Isaiah 42:8.

16. HOW DOES GOD LOOK UPON IDOLATRY?

God looks upon idolatry as degrading, the practice of fools and an abomination in His sight. Acts 17:29; Romans 1:22, 23; Deuteronomy 7:25.

17. WHAT EFFECT DOES IDOLATRY HAVE ON A PERSON'S DESCENDANTS?

God visits His punishment for idolatry on the coming generations of them that hate Him. Exodus 20:5. Note Exodus 32:34, 35.

18. HOW THEN CAN WE PLEASE GOD AND SECURE HIS BLESSINGS?

By serving the only TRUE God and Him only. Exodus 20:6.

19. THE LORD JESUS CHRIST IS THE FULFILLMENT OF THE SECOND COMMANDMENT.

No man could make an image of God that would accurately represent God to man. Jesus' birth among men was God's gift of a satisfactory image. Everything that Jesus did was God being reflected in a living image before mankind. Hebrews 1:3; Romans 8:29; 1 Corinthians 11:7; 15:49; 2 Corinthians 4:4; Colossians 1:15.

20. WHAT IS THE THIRD COMMANDMENT?

"Thou shalt not take the name of the Lord thy God in vain." 20:7.

21. WHAT IS GOD'S NAME?

"God's Name" refers to every name or title by which God has made Himself known; such as, God, LORD, Jehovah, Almighty, Jesus Christ, Holy Ghost, etc. Specifically, it referred to the Scripture's most common name of God the Father, which was "LORD." Note again pages 40-42 of this catechism course for greater detail. Isaiah 42:8; Jeremiah 23:6; Matthew 1:21.

22. WHAT IS USING GOD'S NAME IN VAIN?

Using God's Name in vain is:

[1] Employing any Name of God uselessly, carelessly or in vulgarity; such as, "My God," "Good Lord!" "Jesus Christ," etc. Note the example given in Leviticus 24:10-16, 23.

[2] Cursing, swearing, using witchcraft, lying or deceiving by His Name.

CURSING: "Blaspheming God by speaking evil of Him or mocking Him." Matthew 27:39-43; 2 Kings 18:28-35; 19:21, 22. Also means, "Calling down the anger and punishment of God upon any person or thing." James 3:9, 10; Matthew 26:74; 27:25; 1 Samuel 17:43.

SWEARING by God's Name is taking an oath in which we call upon God to witness the truth of what we say or promise and to punish us if we lie or break our promise. 2 Corinthians 1:23; Deuteronomy 6:13; Hebrews 6:16; Genesis 24:3; Swearing is sinful that is done falsely, thoughtlessly, or in sinful, uncertain or unimportant matters. Matthew 5:33-37; Leviticus 19:12; Matthew 26:72.

USING WITCHCRAFT by God's Name is: using God's Name in order to perform supernatural things, with the help of the devil, such as conjuring, fortunetelling and consulting the dead. Dueteronomy 18:10-12; note the Egyptian sorcerers, Exodus 7 and 8.

LYING AND DECEIVING by God's Name is:

A. Teaching false doctrine and saying that it is God's Word or revelation (false prophets). Matthew 15:9; Jeremiah 23:31; Deuteronomy 12:32; 1 Kings 13:11-19.

B. Covering up an unbelieving heart or a sinful life by a show of piety (hyprocrites). Matthew 15:8; 7:21; 23:13-33; Acts 5:1-11.

81

23. WHAT DOES GOD REQUIRE OF US IN THE THIRD COMMANDMENT?
    The names and titles of God should be used carefully, prayerfully and with the best religious meaning.

24. THE LORD JESUS CHRIST IS THE FULFILLMENT OF THE THIRD COMMANDMENT.
    Since all men have sinned, none could really use the Name of the LORD without bringing some reproach upon it. Jesus, therefore, came "in my Father's Name" (John 5:43; 10:25) to fulfil perfectly the proper use of the Name of God. He also opens to us the free opportunities of that Name. John 15:16; 16:23, 24, 26.

    Many references in the New Testament show that the early Church made great use of the full Name of God. Acts 2:36; Philippians 2:9, 10; Colossians 3:17.

    In water baptism the Name of the Father and of the Son and of the Holy Ghost — "THE LORD-JESUS-CHRIST" — is put upon the new convert. Romans 6:3; 13:14; Galatians 3:27. He becomes a CHRISTian and lives a life that does not make vain use of God's Name.

25. WHAT IS THE FOURTH COMMANDMENT?
    "Remember the Sabbath day, to keep it holy" Exodus 20:8.

26. WHAT DID GOD MEAN BY "THE SABBATH DAY"?
    The Hebrew word "Sabbath" means rest. In Genesis we find that God rested from His labors on the 7th day, so He set it apart and hallowed it. Now, in this commandment, God tells Israel that the 7th day was to be a day of rest, in which no secular work was to be done, and which was to be kept holy to God. There are many Old Testament references. Exodus 16:23-29; 31:14-16; Leviticus 23; Deuteronomy 5:12-15; Nehemiah 13:15-22.

27. DID JESUS KEEP THE SABBATH ACCORDING TO THE LAW?
    No. Jesus violated the Sabbath, as far as the thinking of the Jews was concerned. Matthew 12:2; John 9:16. In fact, it was Jesus' open disregard for their concept of a holy Sabbath that raised His greatest opposition. Matthew 12:1-12; Mark 1:21; 2:23-28; 3:2-5; Luke 6:1-11; 13:10-16; 14:1-5; John 5:9-18; 7:22-23; 9:14-16.

28. HOW DID JESUS FULFILL THE FOURTH COMMANDMENT?
    Jesus fulfilled the Sabbath Law by completely ceasing from His own labors and absolutely resting in God's will. That is why He felt it was possible to profane the Sabbath, but still be blameless (Matthew 12:5); He declared that it IS lawful to DO WELL on the Sabbath days (Matthew 12:12); He felt that the Sabbath was made for the convenience of man in doing God's will, not man for the convenience of an inflexible law (Mark 2:27); He

82

emphasized that the Son of Man is Lord or master of the Sabbath, so that he can control the happenings of that day for the glory of God. Matthew 12:8.

NOTE: Hebrews 3:18; 4:1, 3, 4, 5, 8, 9, 10, 11. This rest from our wills to do the will of God is our Sabbath. Note verse 9, where the word in the original Greek actually refers to the Sabbath!

29. WHEN NON-JEWS WERE CONVERTED AND ADDED TO THE CHRISTIAN CHURCH IN BIBLE DAYS, WERE THEY OBLIGATED TO KEEP THE SEVENTH DAY AS A SABBATH?

The early (Jewish) Apostles settled the matter once and for all in the first epistle written to the Gentiles (Acts 15:23-29). Only FOUR things were required. Note that circumcision, Sabbath-keeping, abstinence from meats, etc., were NOT listed!

30. DOES GOD REQUIRE THAT CHRISTIANS OBSERVE THE SABBATH (SATURDAY) AND OTHER HOLY DAYS OF THE OLD TESTAMENT?

He does not; for in the New Testament, the Sabbath and other holy days were abolished by God Himself. Matthew 12:8; Colossians 2:16, 17.

31. DID GOD COMMAND US CHRISTIANS TO OBSERVE ANY DAY?

God did not command us to observe any day. Romans 14:5, 6; Galatians 4:10, 11.

32. WHY THEN DO WE OBSERVE SUNDAY AND OTHER CHRISTIAN DAYS?

We observe Sunday and other church festivals in order to have time and opportunity for public worship. Hebrews 10:25; Acts 2:42; 1 Corinthians 11:20, 33; 14:19, 23, 26, 28, 33, 34.

The early Christians observed the first day of the week (Sunday). Acts 20:7; 1 Corinthians 16:2. The first day of the week, of course, was known as the day of Christ's resurrection from the dead.

33. WHEN DO WE SIN AGAINST THE FOURTH COMMANDMENT?

Today's Christian sins against the Fourth Commandment when he does not allow each day to be dedicated to the will of God. Also, if he does not utilize the days set aside for public worship in the local church, he robs himself of the worship, the sacraments and the Word of God that he MUST have. Hebrews 13:17; Galatians 6:6, 7; 1 Thessalonians 2:13.

LESSON 6 STUDY QUESTIONS BASED ON
"THE MOSAIC COVENANT"
(The First Table of the Law, 1-4)

1. What are the Ten Commandments?
2. How did God give the Law?

LESSON 6 STUDY QUESTIONS BASED ON
"THE MOSAIC COVENANT"
(The First Table of the Law, 1-4 Continued)

3. With what did the First Table of the Law have to do?
4. With what did the Second Table of the Law have to do?
5. What is the summary of all the Commandments?
6. To whom does God refer when He says "Thou shalt" in the Commandments?
7. What is the First Commandment?
8. What does God require of us in the First Commandment?
9. What does God forbid in the First Commandment?
10. When do men have other gods?
11. Is Jesus Christ another god?
12. How is the Lord Jesus Christ the fulfillment of the First Commandment?

13. What is the Second Commandment?
14. What does this mean?
15. Why does God forbid idolatry in any form or fashion?
16. How does God look upon idolatry?
17. What effect does idolatry have on a person's descendants?
18. How then can we please God and secure His blessings?
19. How does the Lord Jesus Christ fulfill the Second Commandment?

20. What is the Third Commandment?
21. What is God's Name?
22. What is using God's Name in vain?
23. What does God require of us in the Third Commandment?
24. How does the Lord Jesus Christ fulfill the Third Commandment?

25. What is the Fourth Commandment?
26. What did God mean by "The Sabbath Day"?
27. Did Jesus keep the Sabbath according to the Law?
28. How did Jesus fulfill the Fourth Commandment?
29. When non-Jews were converted and added to the Christian Church in Bible days, were they obligated to keep the Seventh Day as a Sabbath?
30. Does God require that we Christians of the New Testament observe the Sabbath (Saturday) and other holy days of the Old Testament?
31. Did God command us Christians to observe any day?
32. Why then do we observe Sunday and other Christian days?
33. When do we sin against the Fourth Commandment?

LESSON 7: THE MOSAIC COVENANT — THE SECOND TABLE OF THE LAW

1. **WHAT IS THE SUMMARY OF THE SECOND TABLE OF THE LAW?**
   "Thou shalt love thy neighbor as thyself." Matthew 22:39.

2. **WHO IS OUR NEIGHBOR?**
   Our neighbor is every one of our fellow men. Jesus' classic answer to this question is found in Luke 10:29-37; there Jesus indicates that "showing compassion to the undeserving" is the way to be a good neighbor. Also, Galatians 6:10; Matthew 5:44; 7:12.

3. <u>WHAT IS THE FIFTH COMMANDMENT?</u>
   "Honor thy Father and thy Mother: that thy days may be long upon the land which the Lord thy God giveth thee." Exodus 20:12.

4. **WHAT DOES THIS MEAN?**
   We should recognize the authority that God has allowed our parents and masters to have. Our fear and love of God should be such that we automatically give honor, service and obedience to our leaders, and hold them in love and esteem.

5. **WHAT DOES GOD FORBID IN THE FIFTH COMMANDMENT?**
   God forbids us to despise our parents and other superiors by disregarding their dignity or provoking them to just anger by disobedience or by any other kind of wickedness. Proverbs 30:17; Romans 13:2. Note sons of Eli, 1 Samuel 2:12, 23, 25; Absolom's rebellion, 2 Samuel 15.

6. **WHAT DOES GOD REQUIRE OF US IN THE FIFTH COMMANDMENT?**
   God requires us:
   A. To honor our parents and other superiors, that is, to regard them as God's representatives. Ephesians 6:2, 3; Leviticus 19:32; Joseph, Genesis 46:29; Solomon, 1 Kings 2:19; Elisha, 2 Kings 2:12.

   B. To serve our parents and other superiors by gladly doing for them what we can. 1 Timothy 5:4. Joseph, Genesis 47:11; Jesus, John 19:26.

   C. To obey our parents and other superiors in all things in which God has placed them over us. Colossians 3:20; Proverbs 23:22; 1 Peter 2:18; Acts 5:29; Jesus, Luke 2:51; Jonathan, 1 Samuel 20:31-33.

   D. To love and esteem our parents and superiors as precious gifts of God.

7. **WHY DOES GOD ADD THE PROMISE "THAT IT MAY BE WELL WITH THEE AND THOU MAYEST LIVE LONG ON THE EARTH?**
   By this promise God impresses upon us the importance and benefit of honoring our parents and superiors and urges us to obey this commandment willingly.

8. HOW IS THE FIFTH COMMANDMENT FULFILLED BY CHRISTIANS?
   A. As regarding the family:
   "Children, obey your parents IN THE LORD" (Ephesians 6:1) indicates that our obedience is to transcend that of the Old Law, for we are to be "in the Lord" — that is, in the very life of Jesus so that we truly love and obey from the heart. 1 Timothy 5 gives some excellent advice about consideration to be shown widows and parents.

   B. As regarding the Church:
   "Rebuke not an elder, but intreat him as a father . . . let the elders that rule well be counted worthy of double honor . . . against an elder receive not an accusation . . . ." 1 Timothy 5:1, 17, 19.

   C. As regarding job superiors:
   "Do them service" — is the theme of 1 Timothy 6:1-3.

9. WHAT IS THE SIXTH COMMANDMENT?
   "Thou shalt not kill." Exodus 20:13.

10. WHAT DOES GOD FORBID IN THE SIXTH COMMANDMENT?
    A. God forbids us to take the life of a fellow man (murder) or our own life (suicide). Genesis 9:6; Matthew 26:52; Romans 13:4.

    B. God forbids us to hurt or harm our neighbor in his body, that is, to do or say anything which may destroy, shorten or embitter his life. Romans 12:19.

    C. God forbids us to bear anger and hatred in our hearts against our neighbor. Matthew 5:22; 15:19; 1 John 3:15; Ephesians 4:26.

11. WHAT DOES GOD REQUIRE OF US IN THE SIXTH COMMANDMENT?
    A. We should help and befriend our neighbor in every bodily need. Romans 12:20; Abraham, Genesis 14:12-16; David, 1 Samuel 26:1-12; The Good Samaritan, Luke 10:33-35.

    B. We should be merciful, kind and forgiving towards our neighbor. Matthew 5:5, 7, 9; 5:25; 6:15; Ephesians 4:32.

12. HOW DID JESUS TEACH US TO FULFILL THE SIXTH COMMANDMENT?
    Matthew 5:21-26. Jesus here teaches that we not only fulfill the Sixth Commandment by NOT committing physical violence, BUT ALSO by not allowing anger and murderous thoughts in our hearts. In other words, the New Covenant of Jesus stops the external sin by going to the very root of the problem in the heart and destroying it.

13. WHAT IS THE SEVENTH COMMANDMENT?
    "Thou shalt not commit adultery." Exodus 20:14.

14. WHAT DOES THIS MEAN?

We should love and fear God in such a way that we live a chaste and decent married life in word and deed, each one loving and honoring his spouse.

15. WHAT IS MARRIAGE?

Marriage was instituted by God to be a lifelong union between one man and one woman unto one flesh. Marriage should follow rightful betrothal or engagement.

"They are no more twain, but one flesh, what therefore God hath joined together let not man put asunder." Matthew 19:6.

The institution of marriage — Genesis 2:18-24; The Angel calls Mary, who was engaged to Joseph, Joseph's wife and calls Joseph her husband — Matthew 1:19, 20, 24.

16. WHAT DOES GOD FORBID IN THE SEVENTH COMMANDMENT?

A. God forbids the breaking of the marriage vow by unfaithfulness or desertion. He permits the innocent party to procure a divorce when the other party is guilty of fornication. Matthew 19:6, 9; Hebrews 13:4; David's adultery, 2 Samuel 11; Herod, Mark 6:18.

B. God also forbids all unchaste and unclean thoughts, desires, words and deeds. Matthew 15:19; 5:28; Ephesians 5:3, 4, 12; Potiphar's wife, Genesis 39:7-12; Samson, Judges 16:1.

17. WHAT IS GOD'S BASIC THOUGHT IN THE SEVENTH COMMANDMENT?

God forbids His people to misuse sex.

18. WHY DOES THIS COMMANDMENT TEACH US TO BE PURE AND MODEST IN BODY?

Our bodies are temples of the Holy Spirit and we should therefore respect them, modestly clothe them, and carefully tend them as befitting the habitation of the true and living God. Romans 12:1; 1 Corinthians 3:16.

19. HERE ARE SOME THINGS THAT WILL ENDANGER OUR CHASTITY:

Idleness, bad companions, drinking, immodest dress, impure conversations, dirty jokes, looking at bad pictures, indecent books and films, and touching one's own body or that of another without necessity simply to satisfy sinful curiosity.

20. WHAT MUST WE DO TO LEAD A CHASTE AND DECENT LIFE?

In the fear of God we must:

A. FIGHT TO OVERCOME all impure thoughts and desires through God's Word and prayer, work and temperance. Genesis 39:9; Psalms 51:10; Proverbs 23:31-33; 1 Corinthians 10:13.

B. FLEE AND AVOID every opportunity for unchasteness.
1 Corinthians 6:18 — "Flee fornication."
2 Timothy — 2:22 — "Flee also youthful lusts."
1 Corinthians 6:19 — "Your body is the temple of the Holy Ghost."
Proverbs 1:10 — "If sinners entice thee, consent thou not."

21. DOES GOD EVER FORBID MARRIAGE?

God never forbids marriage, for He instituted it. Any church that forbids marriage to any of its people is being misled by a doctrine of devils. 1 Timothy 4:3; Hebrews 13:4. In Matthew 19:12 there is a reference to some of God's people who willingly forgo marriage that they might better serve God. 1 Corinthians 9:5.

NOTE: God does forbid a Christian to marry an unbeliever. 2 Corinthians 6:14. The above question and answer is not concerned with REmarriage.

22. WHAT IS ADULTERY ACCORDING TO THE NEW TESTAMENT?

This may seem strange, but the teaching of Jesus on the subject is both more merciful and yet more severe than anything under the Law.

Its severity . . .
Matthew 5:27, 28 quotes the Old Law and the New Law. Under Moses it was a physical sex act that adulterated the marriage contract; under Jesus, the very thought of the heart can adulterate one's standing with God.

Its mercy . . .
John 8 shows a woman caught in the very act being forgiven by Jesus, and told not to continue in such sinning; Moses' Law would have had the woman stoned to death. John 4:17, 18 shows how Jesus dealt with a woman living in sin.

23. WHAT DOES GOD REQUIRE OF MARRIED PEOPLE ESPECIALLY?

God requires married people to love and honor each other, the husband his wife as his God-given helpmate and the wife her husband as her God-given head. Ephesians 5:24, 25.

24. WHAT IS THE EIGHTH COMMANDMENT?

"Thou shalt not steal." Exodus 20:15.

25. WHAT DOES THIS MEAN?

We should fear and love God in such a way that we do not claim for ourselves what rightfully belongs to another.

26. WHAT PARTICULAR SIN DOES GOD FORBID IN THE EIGHTH COMMANDMENT?

God forbids every kind of robbery, theft and fraud, as well as sinful longing for anything that belongs to our neighbor. Ephesians 4:28; Leviticus 19:35;

Jeremiah 22:13; 2 Thessalonians 3:10; Psalms 37:31; Proverbs 29:24.

27. WHAT DOES GOD REQUIRE OF US IN THE EIGHTH COMMANDMENT?
   A. We should help our neighbor to improve and protect his property and business. Exodus 23:4; Matthew 7:12; Romans 13:8-10.
   B. We should help him in every need. Matthew 5:42; Proverbs 19:17; Hebrews 13:16.
   C. We should rejoice when we see him prosper. 1 Corinthians 13:4, 5.

28. WHEN A CHILD OF GOD DESIRES TO STEAL, WHAT WRONG ATTITUDE IS INVOLVED?
   God has promised to supply all of our NEED according to His riches in glory by Christ Jesus, Philippians 4:19. God will never allow His child to lack the basic essentials of life. Note 3 John 2. Therefore, the desire to take another's belongings indicates a lack of trust that God is able to care properly for us. Dishonest action must not replace our love for others and our trust in God's provision.

29. WHAT IS THE NINTH COMMANDMENT?
   "Thou shalt not bear false witness against thy neighbor." Exodus 20:16.

30. WHAT DOES GOD FORBID IN THE NINTH COMMANDMENT?

   A. God forbids us to make any untrue statement against our neighbor in court. Proverbs 19:5; Matthew 26:59-61; 1 Kings 21:13.
   B. God forbids us to belie our neighbor; that is, to lie about him or lie to him or withhold from him the truth in order to harm. Proverbs 19:5; Ephesians 4:25.
   C. God forbids us to betray our neighbor; that is, to reveal his secrets. Proverbs 11:13.
   D. God forbids us to slander or defame our neighbor; that is, to speak evil of him and thus injure or destroy his good name. James 4:11; Psalms 50:19-22; Luke 6:37; Matthew 18:15.
   E. God forbids us to have evil thoughts against our neighbor or to plot against him. Zechariah 8:17.

31. WHAT IS FALSE WITNESS?
   Every evil report about your neighbor that cannot be legally proven is false witness.

32. HOW SHOULD A CHRISTIAN DEAL WITH ONE WHO IS INVOLVED IN EVIL?
   Matthew 18:15-17. We are always to deal with the individual himself, and

not secretly to speak ill of him to others. If the one in error is a Christian who will not correct the problem, take others also to confirm your conviction. Finally, if there is no repentance of a legally confirmed sin, let the individual be excommunicated. 1 Timothy 5:19 safeguards the elders against false witness.

33. WHAT IS THE TENTH COMMANDMENT?

"Thou shalt not covet thy neighbor's house, thou shalt not covet thy neighbor's wife, nor his manservant, nor his maidservant, nor his ox, nor his ass, nor anything that is thy neighbor's." Exodus 20:17.

34. WHAT DOES THIS MEAN?

We should fear and love God that we not craftily seek to get our neighbor's inheritance or house. We should not estrange, force or entice away from our neighbor his wife, servants or cattle, but urge them to stay and do their duty. Isaiah 5:8; Matthew 23:14; 1 Timothy 6:8-10. Note how Ahab coveted Naboth's vineyard, 1 Kings 21:1-16; David coveted the wife of Uriah, 2 Samuel 11:2-4; Absolom estranged the hearts of the people from David, 2 Samuel 15:1-6.

35. WHAT DOES GOD REQUIRE OF US IN THE TENTH COMMANDMENT?

God requires that our hearts be filled with holy desires toward our neighbor.

36. HOLY DESIRES WILL MOTIVATE US IN WHAT WAYS?

Such holy desires will move us to urge our neighbor's wife and servants to stay with him and to do their duty. It will move us to help our neighbor and be of service to him in keeping his inheritance or house. "By love serve one another." Galatians 5:13.

37. WHAT DOES GOD PARTICULARLY IMPRESS UPON US IN THE LAST COMMANDMENT?

God impresses upon us:

A. That in His sight evil desire, or lust, is indeed sin and deserves condemnation. Romans 7:7; James 1:14, 15.

B. That we should not have any evil lust whatever in our hearts, but only holy desires and love of God and of all that is good. Leviticus 19:2; Matthew 5:48; Psalms 37:4.

LESSON 7 STUDY QUESTIONS BASED ON "THE MOSAIC COVENANT" (The Second Table of the Law, 5-10)

1. What is the summary of the Second Table of the Law?
2. Who is our neighbor?

3. What is the Fifth Commandment?
4. What does this mean?
5. What does God forbid in the Fifth Commandment?
6. What does God require of us in the Fifth Commandment?
7. Why does God add the promise "That it may be well with thee and thou mayest live long on the earth?
8. How is the Fifth Commandment fulfilled by Christians?

9. What is the Sixth Commandment?
10. What does God forbid in the Sixth Commandment?
11. What does God require of us in the Sixth Commandment?
12. How did Jesus teach us to fulfill the Sixth Commandment?

13. What is the Seventh Commandment?
14. What does this mean?
15. What is marriage?
16. What does God forbid in the Seventh Commandment?
17. What is God's basic thought in the Seventh Commandment?
18. Why does this commandment teach us to be pure and modest in body?
19. What are some things that will endanger our chastity?
20. What must we do to lead a chaste and decent life?
21. Does God ever forbid marriage?
22. What is adultery according to the New Testament?
23. What does God require of married people especially?

24. What is the Eighth Commandment?
25. What does this mean?
26. What particular sin does God forbid in the Eighth Commandment?
27. What does God require of us in the Eighth Commandment?
28. When a child of God desires to steal, what wrong attitude is involved?

29. What is the Ninth Commandment?
30. What does God forbid in the Ninth Commandment?
31. What is false witness?
32. How should a Christian deal with one who is involved in evil?

33. What is the Tenth Commandment?
34. What does this mean?
35. What does God require of us in the Tenth Commandment?
36. Holy desires will motivate us in what ways?
37. What does God particularly impress upon us in the last commandment?

LESSON 8: THE DAVIDIC COVENANT (DAVID AND THE ETERNAL THRONE)

1. WHY IS DAVID CONSIDERED TO BE IMPORTANT?

    David is one of the most prominent figures in the history of the world; a mountain peak among Bible characters. He is the most famous ancestor of Christ. Jesus is not called the Son of Abraham, or the Son of Jacob, but the Son of David; as, Matthew 21:9.

2. WHAT WAS THE CHIEF CHARACTERISTIC OF DAVID?

    Many things could be said of David; he was a fine athlete, a courageous warrior, a military genius, a shrewd politician, an outstanding musician, etc.

    David's chief characteristic, however, was that "He was a man after God's own heart." 1 Samuel 13:14. This means that he had a sensitive soul that hungered to do God's will. He was a worshipper.

3. WHAT IS THE MAIN THOUGHT OF THE DAVIDIC COVENANT?

    God promised David that his house would have an eternal throne and dominion.

4. DID THIS COVENANT JUST INVOLVE DAVID'S NATURAL DESCENDANTS?

    The Davidic Covenant referred to the natural descendants, but made provision for a spiritual fulfillment through Christ when the natural throne fell into sin.

5. WHERE DO WE FIND THE RECORD OF THE DAVIDIC COVENANT?

    2 Samuel 7; 1 Chronicles 17; also, there are references made to the Davidic Covenant in the book of Psalms.

6. LISTED BELOW ARE THE SEVEN MAIN THOUGHTS OF THE DAVIDIC COVENANT.

    As New Testament references are used along with the Old, it becomes quite apparent that God actually intended for the Davidic Covenant to find its fulfillment in the Lord Jesus Christ and the Church.

    A. "I WILL MAKE THEE A GREAT NAME." 2 Samuel 7:9; 1 Chronicles 17:8; note the many Scripture references in your concordance on "David"; also, Christ's Name — Hebrews 1:3; Matthew 1:21; Acts 2:36; 3:6, 16.

    B. "AND I WILL APPOINT A PLACE FOR MY PEOPLE ISRAEL, AND WILL PLANT THEM, THAT THEY MAY DWELL IN THEIR OWN PLACE, AND BE MOVED NO MORE." 2 Samuel 7:10; 1 Chronicles 17:9; Jeremiah 23:5, 6. Revelation 3:7 shows Christ with power to admit or shut out individuals from the City of David, the New Jerusalem, the Messianic Kingdom. Isaiah 22:22.

    C. ISRAEL WOULD NO LONGER BE WASTED BY ENEMIES, AND GOD SAYS, "I WILL SUBDUE ALL THINE ENEMIES." 2 Samuel

7:10, 11; 1 Chronicles 17:9; Luke 1:71; Revelation 5:5; 22:5. It is the "Root of David" who prevails!

D. "THE LORD WILL BUILD THEE AN HOUSE." 2 Samuel 7:11; 1 Chronicles 17:10; Luke 1:69.

E. THE SEED OF DAVID WOULD BUILD AN HOUSE FOR GOD'S NAME, AND "I WILL ESTABLISH THE THRONE OF HIS KINGDOM FOR EVER." 2 Samuel 7:12, 13; 1 Chronicles 17:12; Psalms 132:11; Luke 1:32; Acts 2:30; 2 Timothy 2:8; Hebrews 1:8; The throne is established by resurrection power!

F. "I WILL BE HIS FATHER AND HE SHALL BE MY SON: AND I WILL NOT TAKE MY MERCY AWAY FROM HIM." 2 Samuel 7:14, 15; 1 Chronicles 17:13; Isaiah 7:14; 9:6-7; Micah 5:2; Luke 1:30-35; 72, Hebrews 1:5; Acts 13:34; Hebrews 2:14, 18.

G. "THE SEED TO BE SETTLED IN THE HOUSE, THE KINGDOM AND THE THRONE FOREVER." 2 Samuel 7:16; 1 Chronicles 17:14; Isaiah 9:7; Psalms 89:29, 36, 37; 45:6; Luke 1:33; Hebrews 3:6; 8:1, 2.

7. DAVID'S TABERNACLE (OR, HOUSE) FINDS FULFILLMENT IN CHRIST'S CHURCH.
Link Acts 15:15-17 with Amos 9:11, 12. The Apostle James used a peculiar Scripture to verify that God was really accepting the converted heathen Gentiles into the Church. The Holy Ghost confirmed this as the truth (15:28). David's House of Praise is restored in the Church and David's Throne is the Heavenly Throne of Christ.

LESSON 8 STUDY QUESTIONS BASED ON
"THE DAVIDIC COVENANT"

1. Why is David considered to be important?
2. What was the chief characteristic of David?
3. What is the main thought of the Davidic Covenant?
4. Did this convenant just involve David's natural descendants?
5. Where do we find the record of the Davidic Covenant?
6. Can you list the seven main thoughts of the Davidic Covenant?
7. How does David's Tabernacle find fulfillment in Christ's Church?

PART V.
THE LIFE AND MINISTRY OF JESUS CHRIST

PART V. THE LIFE AND MINISTRY OF JESUS CHRIST

SECTION V. THE LIFE AND MINISTRY OF JESUS CHRIST

PLEASE NOTE: We now begin the last major part of the Catechism. In the previous Section we studied the six major covenants mentioned in the Old Testament. The rest of this Course will be a detailed study of God's last covenant with mankind — the New Covenant of our Lord and Saviour Jesus Christ. The Sacraments and experiences of the Church will be carefully examined as the fulfillment of this Covenant. And, of course, since Jesus Himself is the very heart of the New Covenant, we will study what He has done, is doing now and what He will yet accomplish in the Church.

LESSON 1: THE DISPENSATION OF GRACE

1. WHAT DOES "GRACE" MEAN?
   "Grace" means unmerited favor or undeserved kindness.

2. WHAT IS THE DISPENSATION OF GRACE?
   The Dispensation of Grace is this present period of time in which "the kindness and love of God our Saviour toward man" is extended. This period of time is sometimes called the Church Age or Dispensation of the Holy Spirit. Titus 3:4, 5; Romans 3:21, 22. Refer to the Dispensational Chart on page 58.

3. WHAT IS THE PURPOSE FOR THE DISPENSATION OF GRACE?

   Under the Dispensation of the Law God demanded righteousness from man; under the Dispensation of Grace, God gives righteousness to man.

   The purpose, then, for the Dispensation of Grace is to impute righteousness to man whereby he can have fellowship with God. Romans 8:3,4; Philippians 3:9; Ephesians 2:8, 9.

4. HOW DOES THIS DISPENSATION OF GRACE DIFFER FROM THE DISPENSATION OF LAW?

   A. Law is connected with Moses and works; Grace with Christ and faith. John 1:17; Romans 10:4-10.

   B. The Law blesses the good; Grace saves the bad. Exodus 19:5; Ephesians 2:1-9.

   C. Law demands that blessings be earned; Grace is a free gift. Deuteronomy 28:1-6; Ephesians 2:8, 9; Romans 4:4, 5.

5. WHAT IS THE TEST THAT GOD PUTS TO MAN DURING THIS DISPENSATION OF GRACE?
   The test is no longer legal obedience, as condition of salvation, but the acceptance or rejection of Christ, with good works as a fruit of salvation. John 1:12, 13; 3:36.

97

6. WHAT HAS BEEN THE RESULT OF THIS TEST?

> The immediate result of this testing was the rejection of Christ by the Jews, and His crucifixion by Jew and Gentile. Acts 4:27.

> Churches which profess Christ but do not possess Him respond to the test of Grace by going into apostasy. 2 Timothy 3:1-8.

> The glorious end result will be an overcoming Church filled with God. Colossians 1:27; Ephesians 3:16-21.

LESSON 1 STUDY QUESTIONS BASED ON
"THE DISPENSATION OF GRACE"

1. What does "grace" mean?
2. What is the Dispensation of Grace?
3. What is the purpose for the Dispensation of Grace?
4. How does this Dispensation of Grace differ from the Dispensation of the Law?
5. What is the test that God puts to man during this Dispensation of Grace?
6. What has been the result of this test?

LESSON 2: JESUS, THE CHRIST

1. WHO IS JESUS CHRIST?

Jesus Christ is true God and also true man; or, it may be said that Jesus Christ is truly both God and man.

2. WHAT TWO EXPRESSIONS CLEARLY SHOW THE DIVINE AND HUMAN NATURES OF JESUS?

Since he was begotten by God the Father,
Jesus Christ is called "The Son of God."
Since he was born of the Virgin Mary,
Jesus Christ is called "The Son of Man."

3. WHY DO WE BELIEVE THAT JESUS CHRIST IS TRUE GOD?

We believe that Jesus Christ is true God because the Scriptures ascribe to him:

A. DIVINE NAMES:
   1 John 5:20 — "the TRUE God"
   John 20:28 — "My Lord and my God"
   Matthew 17:5 — "My Beloved Son"
   Romans 9:5 — "Christ came, who is over all, God"
   Acts 20:28 — "God hath purchased"

B. DIVINE ATTRIBUTES:
   John 1:1, 2 — Eternal
   Hebrews 13:8 — Unchangeable
   Matthew 28:20 — Ever-present
   John 21:17 — Omniscient
   Matthew 28:18 — Omnipotent

C. DIVINE WORKS:
   John 1:3 — Creation
   Hebrews 1:3 — Preservation
   Matthew 9:6 — Forgives sins
   John 5:27 — Judgment

   NOTE: The four Gospels record that Jesus performed 17 bodily cures, 9 miracles over the forces of nature, 6 cures of demoniacs and raised 3 people from the dead!

D. DIVINE HONOR AND GLORY:
   John 5:23 — The Son is to be honored even as the Father
   Hebrews 1:6 — The angels are to worship the Son
   Hebrews 1:8 — "Thy throne, O God, is for ever and ever"
   Titus 2:13 — The Glorious Appearing

99

LESSON 2: JESUS, THE CHRIST (Continued)

4. WHY DO WE BELIEVE THAT JESUS CHRIST IS TRUE MAN?
   We believe that Jesus Christ is also true man because the Scriptures:

   A. EXPRESSLY CALL HIM MAN:
      1 Timothy 2:5 — "the man Christ Jesus"

   B. ASCRIBE TO HIM A HUMAN BODY AND SOUL:
      Luke 24:39 — "Behold my hands and feet"
      Matthew 26:38 — "My soul is exceeding sorrowful"
      Hebrews 10:5 — "a body hast thou prepared me"

   C. ASCRIBE TO HIM HUMAN FEELINGS AND ACTIONS:
      Jesus slept (Mark 4:38), hungered (Matthew 4:2), thirsted (John 19:28), wearied (John 4:6), wept (John 11:35) and suffered and died (Matthew 26 and 27).

5. WHAT TWO NATURES, THEN, ARE UNITED IN CHRIST?
   The Divine and the human natures are united in Christ, both natures together forming one undivided and indivisible person (personal union).

   John 1:14 — "The Word was made flesh. . the only-begotten"
   Colossians 2:9 — "In Him dwelleth all the fulness of the Godhead bodily"
   Isaiah 9:6 — "A child is born . . . a Son is given"
   Matthew 28:18 — "All power is given unto Me in heaven and in earth"

6. WHY WAS IT NECESSARY FOR OUR SAVIOUR TO BE TRUE MAN?
   It was necessary for our Saviour to be true man:

   A. THAT HE MIGHT TAKE OUR PLACE UNDER THE LAW:
      Galatians 4:4, 5 — "Made of a woman, made under the Law, to redeem"

   B. THAT HE MIGHT BE ABLE TO SUFFER AND DIE IN OUR STEAD:
      Hebrews 2:14 — "He also Himself likewise took part of the same"

7. WHY WAS IT NECESSARY FOR OUR SAVIOUR TO BE TRUE GOD?
   It was necessary for our Saviour to be true God:

   A. THAT HIS FULFILLING OF THE LAW MIGHT BE SUFFICIENT FOR ALL MEN. Psalms 49:7, 8; Romans 5:19.

   B. THAT HIS LIFE AND DEATH MIGHT BE SUFFICIENT RANSOM FOR OUR REDEMPTION. Mark 10:45.

   C. THAT HE MIGHT BE ABLE TO OVERCOME DEATH AND THE DEVIL FOR US. 2 Timothy 1:10; Hebrews 2:14; 1 Corinthians 15:57.

8. WHAT DO WE MEAN WHEN WE CALL JESUS "THE CHRIST"?
CHRIST means "the CHRISTened One" or "the Anointed One." The Hebrew word for Christ is Messiah. In the Old Testament period, prophets, priests and kings were anointed with oil for their public ministries.

Jesus was anointed, not with oil, but with the Holy Spirit without measure!

9. FOR WHAT THREEFOLD OFFICE WAS CHRIST ANOINTED?
Christ was anointed to be my Prophet, Priest and King.

A. AS MY PROPHET, Jesus revealed perfectly God's will for the redemption of mankind. He proclaimed the message; He was the VOICE of God, the communication. Deuteronomy 18:15; Matthew 17:5; John 1:17, 18; Luke 10:16.

B. AS MY PRIEST, Christ fulfilled the Law in my stead perfectly, sacrificed Himself for me and still intercedes for me with His heavenly Father. Galatians 4:4, 5; 1 Corinthians 15:3; Hebrews 7:26, 27; 1 John 2:1, 2.

C. AS MY KING, Christ with His mighty power rules over all creatures, governs and protects His Church, and finally leads it to glory. Matthew 28:18; John 18:33, 37; 2 Timothy 4:18.

10. WHAT TWO STATES DO WE SEE IN CHRIST'S WORK OF REDEMPTION?
The state of humiliation and the state of exaltation.

LESSON 2 STUDY QUESTIONS BASED ON "JESUS, THE CHRIST"

1. Who is Jesus Christ?
2. What two expressions clearly show the Divine and human natures of Jesus?
3. Give four reasons for our belief that Jesus Christ is true God.
4. Give three reasons for our belief that Jesus Christ is true man.
5. What two natures, then, are united in Christ?
6. Why was it necessary for our Saviour to be true man?
7. Why was it necessary for our Saviour to be true God?
8. What do we mean when we call Jesus "The Christ"?
9. For what threefold office was Christ anointed?
10. What two states do we see in Christ's work of redemption?

THE MINISTRY OF JESUS
HUMILIATION – AND – EXALTATION
John 3:13; 8:14; 16:28

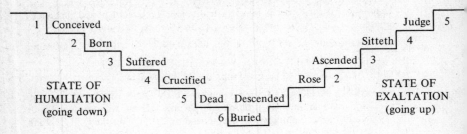

```
1 | Conceived                                              Judge | 5
    2 | Born                                        Sitteth | 4
        3 | Suffered                        Ascended | 3
    STATE OF           4 | Crucified         Rose | 2   STATE OF
    HUMILIATION             5 | Dead  Descended | 1      EXALTATION
    (going down)               6 | Buried                 (going up)
```

LESSON 3: THE SAVIOUR IN THE STATE OF HUMILIATION

1.   WHAT WAS CHRIST'S STATE OF HUMILIATION?
Christ's state of humiliation was made up of this: Jesus Christ did not, in His every day life, always fully use the Divine power that was given Him by His Father but rather became as a man and subjected Himself to the weakness and limitations of man. Philippians 2:5-11; Hebrews 2:14; John 2:11; 11:40; 18:6.

2.   WHAT WAS THE FULL EXTENT OF CHRIST'S HUMILIATION?
He was conceived by the Holy Ghost.
He was born of the Virgin Mary.
He suffered and was persecuted by mankind.
He was crucified.
He died.
He was buried.

3.   WHAT DO THE SCRIPTURES TEACH OF THE CONCEPTION OF CHRIST?
The Bible teaches that the Virgin Mary received the conception of her son, Jesus, by Divine means. The Holy Ghost placed the Seed of God in the seed of woman, causing Divine conception. Mary, representing all mankind, supplied the seed for the flesh and bone of the child to be born; in contrast, the Heavenly Father supplied the seed that would produce the incorruptible blood stream that would give life to the Christ. Luke 1:35; Matthew 1:20.

4.   WHAT DO THE SCRIPTURES TEACH OF THE BIRTH OF CHRIST?
The Scriptures teach that Jesus Christ was born a true man of the Virgin Mary, in Bethlehem of Judea, the city of David. Luke 2.
"Behold, a virgin shall conceive and bear a Son" – Isaiah 7:14.
"Unto us a Child is born, unto us a Son is given" – Isaiah 9:6.
"She brought forth her first-born Son and wrapped him" – Luke 2:7.

5. WHAT DO THE SCRIPTURES TEACH OF THE SUFFERING OF CHRIST?
   The Bible teaches that in His earthly life Jesus Christ suffered poverty, contempt and persecution. Hebrews 2:18; 5:8; 2 Corinthians 8:9; Matthew 8:20; Isaiah 53:3; John 8:40. Swaddling clothes and manger at birth, Luke 2:7; Herod sought to destroy the baby Jesus, Matthew 2:13; rejected at Nazareth, Luke 4:29; in the temple they attempted to stone Him, John 8:59.

6. WHAT DO THE SCRIPTURES TEACH ABOUT THE CRUCIFIXION OF CHRIST?

   A. Under the authority of Pontius Pilate, Christ suffered extreme agony of body and soul. They beat him, then nailed him to a wooden cross where He died. John 19:1-3; 16-18.

   B. David accurately foretold the crucifixion of Jesus. Psalms 22:6-8, 14-16; Psalms 69:17-21.

   C. The cross, as an instrument of death, was cursed by God. "Cursed is everyone that hangeth on a tree" — Galatians 3:13.

7. WHAT DO THE SCRIPTURES TEACH ABOUT THE BURIAL OF CHRIST?

   A. The bodies of crucified criminals were dumped on the garbage pile in the Valley of Hinnon. Jesus, however, made His grave with the rich. The Virgin-born was placed in the virgin tomb that belonged to Joseph.

   B. The body of Jesus was to remain buried for THREE days — this was the sign of the prophet Jonah! Matthew 12:39; Luke 11:29.
      "The Son of man (shall) be 3 days and 3 nights in the heart of the earth." Matthew 12:40.

      NOTE: Jesus was actually crucified on Wednesday, not "Good Friday." During the Passion Week there were actually two Sabbaths: Thursday was a "High Sabbath" (the first day of the Week of Unleavened Bread) and then the regular Sabbath on Saturday. Daniel 9:27; Leviticus 23:8; Numbers 28:18; Exodus 12:16; Mark 14:1; John 19:31.

   C. The Body of Jesus did not see corruption or decay. Acts 13:37.

8. FOR WHAT PURPOSE DID CHRIST UNDERGO THE 6 STEPS OF HUMILIATION?
   Christ so humbled Himself to redeem me, a lost and condemned creature.

9. WHAT IS THE MEANING OF "REDEEM"?
   "Redeem" means to "buy back." You redeem whatever has been pawned; you may save trading stamps and then redeem them, that is, buy back their worth in merchandise. Jesus' life was the ransom price that bought my soul!

10. FROM WHAT HAS CHRIST REDEEMED YOU?
Christ has redeemed me from all sins, from death and from the power of the devil.

11. HOW HAS CHRIST REDEEMED YOU FROM ALL SINS?
A. Christ has taken away all my guilt and suffered all my punishment. Romans 5:19; 2 Corinthians 5:21; John 1:29; Galatians 3:13.

B. Christ has freed me from the slavery of sin. 1 Peter 2:24 and John 8:34, 35.

12. HOW HAS CHRIST REDEEMED YOU FROM DEATH?
Christ has overcome death; now I need not fear temporal death, since eternal death has no power over me. Hebrews 2:14, 15; 1 Corinthians 15:55-57; 2 Timothy 1:10.

13. HOW HAS CHRIST REDEEMED YOU FROM THE POWER OF THE DEVIL?
Christ has overcome the devil and conquered him; therefore, he can no longer successfully accuse me, and I can now overcome his temptations. Genesis 3:15; 1 John 3:8; James 4:7; Colossians 2:15; Romans 8:31-34; Revelation 2:10; 1 Peter 5:8, 9.

14. WITH WHAT HAS CHRIST REDEEMED YOU?
Christ has redeemed me — not with money — but with His holy, precious blood and with His innocent suffering and death. 1 Peter 1:18, 19; 1 John 1:7; Isaiah 53:5.

15. HOW DOES THIS WORK OF REDEMPTION BENEFIT YOU?
As my substitute Christ has atoned or made satisfaction for my sins by paying the penalty of my guilt. 2 Corinthians 5:21; read Isaiah 53:4, 5, making it personal.

16. HAS CHRIST REDEEMED, PURCHASED AND WON ONLY YOU?
Christ has redeemed me and all lost and condemned mankind. 1 Timothy 1:15; Matthew 18:11; John 1:29; 1 John 2:2; 2 Corinthians 5:15.

THIS DOES NOT MEAN THAT ALL MEN WILL BE SAVED, BUT RATHER THAT ALL MEN MAY BE SAVED IF THEY SO DESIRE, FOR THE PRICE HAS BEEN FULLY PAID!

LESSON 3 STUDY QUESTIONS BASED ON
"THE SAVIOUR IN THE STATE OF HUMILIATION"

1. What was Christ's state of humiliation?
2. What was the full extent of Christ's humiliation?

3. What do the Scriptures teach of the conception of Christ?
4. What do the Scriptures teach of the birth of Christ?
5. What do the Scriptures teach of the suffering of Christ?
6. What do the Scriptures teach about the crucifixion of Christ?
7. What do the Scriptures teach about the burial of Christ?
8. For what purpose did Christ undergo the six steps of humiliation?
9. What is the meaning of "redeem"?
10. From what has Christ redeemed you?
11. How has Christ redeemed you from all sins?
12. How has Christ redeemed you from death?
13. How has Christ redeemed you from the power of the devil?
14. With what has Christ redeemed you?
15. How does this work of redemption benefit you?
16. Has Christ redeemed, purchased and won only you?

LESSON 4: THE SAVIOUR IN THE STATE OF EXALTATION

1. WHAT WAS CHRIST'S STATE OF EXALTATION?

> Out of Jesus' humiliation and physical death was birthed the ministry that could never die. Through the power of the Holy Spirit, Jesus entered the state of resurrection life which exalted Him above all the power of sin, death, hell and the devil. Philippians 2:9-11; 2 Corinthians 5:19.

2. WHAT DID CHRIST ACCOMPLISH IN HIS STATE OF EXALTATION?

> Christ accomplished this:
>> He descended into hell.
>> After being buried three days, He rose again from the dead.
>> He ascended into heaven and sitteth on the right hand of God, the Father Almighty.
>> From thence He shall come to judge the quick and the dead.

3. WHAT DO THE SCRIPTURES TEACH OF CHRIST'S DESCENT INTO HELL?

> The Bible indicates that while the body of Jesus lay in the tomb, Christ descended by the Spirit into hell (the abode of the dead), not to suffer, but to proclaim victory over His enemies. 1 Peter 3:18, 19.

4. WHAT DO THE SCRIPTURES TEACH OF CHRIST'S RESURRECTION?

> After Christ's body had lain in the tomb for three days, Christ miraculously rose from the dead and came forth from the tomb. He showed Himself alive to His disciples. Luke 24:39; Acts 10:40, 41; 1 Corinthians 15: 4-8; Acts 1:3; Matthew 27:62-66; 28; Mark 16; Luke 24; John 20, 21.

5. WHY IS THE RESURRECTION OF CHRIST OF SUCH IMPORTANCE AND COMFORT TO US?

> Christ's resurrection definitely proves:
>
> A. That Christ is the Son of God. Romans 1:4.
> B. That His doctrine is the truth. John 2:19.
> C. That God the Father has accepted the sacrifice of His Son for the reconciliation of the world. 1 Corinthians 15:17; Romans 4:25.
> D. That all believers shall rise unto eternal life. John 14:19; 11:25,26.

6. WHAT DO THE SCRIPTURES TEACH OF CHRIST'S ASCENSION INTO HEAVEN?

> The Scriptures teach that the Lord Jesus Christ bodily and visibly ascended to heaven and entered into the glory of His Father, as our forerunner. Hebrews 6:20; Ephesians 4:10; John 17:24; 14:3. Read the Bible narrative of Christ's ascension: Luke 24:50, 51; Acts 1:9-11.

7. WHAT DO THE SCRIPTURES TEACH OF CHRIST'S SITTING ON THE RIGHT HAND OF GOD THE FATHER ALMIGHTY?

> The Scriptures teach that the Lord Jesus Christ rules and fills all things with divine power and majesty. Ephesians 1:20-23; Acts 7:55, 56.

8. WHAT COMFORT DO YOU DERIVE FROM CHRIST'S SITTING ON THE RIGHT HAND OF GOD THE FATHER ALMIGHTY?

We derive the comfort that it is Jesus, the Lord of glory and the exalted Christ, who . . .

A. AS OUR PROPHET, sends men to preach the Gospel of redemption and also guides the Church on to perfection. Ephesians 4:10-12; Luke 10:16.

B. AS OUR PRIEST, intercedes (pleads our cause) for us before God. 1 John 2:1; Romans 8:34.

C. AS OUR KING, governs and protects His Church and as Head of the Church, rules the world in the interest of the Church. Ephesians 1:20-23; Matthew 22:44; Psalms 110:1.

9. WHAT DO THE SCRIPTURES TEACH OF CHRIST'S COMING TO JUDGMENT?

The Scriptures teach that . . .

A. CHRIST SHALL RETURN visibly and in glory. Acts 1:11; Revelation 1:7; Matthew 25:31.

B. HE WILL JUDGE THE WORLD in righteousness by His Word. Acts 10:42; 2 Corinthians 5:10; Acts 17:31; John 12:48.

C. HE WILL COME ON THE LAST DAY, which is appointed by God, but unknown to man. Acts 17:31; Mark 13:32; 2 Peter 3:10; Matthew 24:27; 1 Peter 4:7.

The final judgment — Matthew 25:31-46; Signs preceding Christ's Coming — Matthew 24 and 2 Thessalonians 2.

NOTE: On page 58 we have drawn "God's Plan of the Ages"; observe that the coming of the Lord Jesus Christ occurs as both the climax of the sixth day and the opening of the seventh day.

10. WHAT IS THE PURPOSE OF CHRIST'S ENTIRE WORK OF REDEMPTION?

The purpose of Christ's entire work of redemption is . . .

A. THAT I MAY BE HIS OWN. Through God's wonderful mercy, I am now righteous and blameless in His sight; I am His child, and I belong to Him. Revelation 5:9; 1 Corinthians 6:19.

B. THAT I MAY LIVE UNDER HIM IN HIS KINGDOM, and serve Him in everlasting righteousness, innocence and blessedness; that is, that I willingly serve Him by an active Christian life and enjoy His blessings NOW on earth and HEREAFTER in eternity. Galatians 2:20; Luke

1:74, 75; 2 Corinthians 5:15; Ephesians 2:10; Romans 12:4-16.

C. THAT THE ENTIRE CREATION can find redemption through the Church just as the Church did through her Christ. Romans 8:19; Ephesians 3:9, 10.

LESSON 4 STUDY QUESTIONS BASED ON "THE SAVIOUR IN THE STATE OF EXALTATION"

1. What was Christ's state of exaltation?
2. What did Christ accomplish in His state of exaltation?
3. What do the Scriptures teach of Christ's descent into hell?
4. What do the Scriptures teach of Christ's resurrection?
5. Why is the resurrection of Christ of such importance and comfort to us?
6. What do the Scriptures teach of Christ's ascension into Heaven?
7. What do the Scriptures teach of Christ's sitting on the right hand of God the Father Almighty?
8. What comfort do you derive from Christ's sitting on the right hand of God?
9. What do the Scriptures teach of Christ's coming to judgment?
10. What is the purpose of Christ's entire work of redemption?

PART VI.
THE BENEFITS OF THE CROSS

PART VI. THE BENEFITS OF THE CROSS

PART VI.   THE BENEFITS OF THE CROSS

KEY VERSE: "But he was wounded for our transgressions: he was bruised for our iniquities: the chastisement of our peace was upon him: and with his stripes we are healed." Isaiah 53:5.

1.   WHAT IS MEANT BY THE "BENEFITS" OF THE CROSS?
The benefits of the cross are those gifts which Jesus Christ purchased for me when He died upon the cross of Calvary.

2.   WHAT ARE THESE BENEFITS?
The benefits of the cross are these:

   A.   FORGIVENESS OF SINS AND ETERNAL LIFE —
"wounded for our transgressions"
   B.   DELIVERANCE FROM INBRED INIQUITIES —
"bruised for our iniquities"
   C.   PEACE FOR THE MIND AND HEART —
"the chastisement of our peace"
   D.   HEALING FOR THE BODY —
"with his stripes we are healed"

LESSON 1:   WOUNDED FOR OUR TRANSGRESSIONS

1.   WHY WAS CHRIST WOUNDED FOR OUR SINS?
The Law of God demanded the shedding of blood in order to forgive man's sin ("the wages of sin is death"). Hebrews 9:22.

Jesus Christ became the sacrifice for the sins of mankind; He took our place before God and took the punishment for our sins. 1 Peter 2:24.

2.   WHAT IS MEANT BY FORGIVENESS OF SINS AND ETERNAL LIFE?
Forgiveness comes when the soul is cleansed by the blood of Jesus Christ of all its mistakes, offenses and transgressions against God. Eternal life is to live forever. It is the gift of God to those who believe on the Lord Jesus Christ. Hebrews 9:22; John 5:24; Matthew 26:28.

3.   HOW MAY I HAVE MY SINS FORGIVEN?
Our sins are forgiven and forgotten by God when we confess our sins to Jesus Christ and ask His forgiveness for them. 1 John 1:7, 9; Isaiah 1:18; Psalms 103:12.

4.   HOW CAN I KNOW THAT MY SINS ARE FORGIVEN?
There are TWO ways that we KNOW that our sins are forgiven:

   A.   THE WORD OF GOD SAYS THEY ARE FORGIVEN! 1 John 1:9.

   B.   THE SPIRIT OF GOD WITNESSES IN OUR HEARTS that we are forgiven!   Romans 8:16; 1 John 4:13; 5:10.

111

5. WHAT IS THE WITNESS OF THE SPIRIT?

When we have repented of our sins and accepted Jesus Christ as our personal Saviour, God sends the Spirit of the Son into our hearts as a witness that we are now His children. God's Spirit causes our spirit to cry "abba Father" (an affectionate term) as a witness that we are now His. Mark 14:36; Romans 8:15; Galatians 4:6.

This experience comes AFTER faith, not before. Many people look for the testimony of the Spirit before they accept the testimony of God's written Word. This is an inversion of God's order. Trust in — rely upon — believe on — the bare Word of God. John 1:12.

6. HERE IS A SIMPLE, LOGICAL FORMULA FOR OBTAINING SPIRITUAL THINGS.

First, a person must hear the FACTS. The facts then produce the FAITH in the mind of the hearer. Then, the faith produces the FEELING. This is the formula for obtaining forgiveness, healing or any other blessing from the Word. Romans 10:17.

Remember: FACTS + FAITH = FEELING (do not reverse formula)

LESSON 1 STUDY QUESTIONS BASED ON "WOUNDED FOR OUR TRANSGRESSIONS"

1. What is meant by the "benefits" of the Cross?
2. Name the four main benefits of the Cross?
3. Why was Christ wounded for our sins?
4. What is meant by forgiveness of sins and eternal life?
5. How may I have my sins forgiven?
6. In what two ways can I know that my sins are forgiven?
7. What is the witness of the Spirit?
8. What is the simple, logical formula for obtaining spiritual things?

LESSON 2: BRUISED FOR OUR INIQUITIES

1. WHAT IS INIQUITY? HOW DOES IT DIFFER FROM SIN?
   Iniquity is the evil that is born in us that breeds the transgression. Sin is the actual transgression of the law.

   "were by nature the children of wrath, even as others" — Ephesians 2:3. "death passed upon all men, for that all have sinned" — Romans 5:12.

2. WHAT IS MEANT BY "BRUISED FOR OUR INIQUITIES"?
   Jesus Christ suffered actual physical hurt. "Buffet" in Matthew 26:67 means "to strike with savage force with the clenched fist." At Pilate's command, Jesus was also "scourged" (Matthew 27:26).

   "Scourging usually preceded capital punishment . . . Scourging was done with a whip which was made of a number of leather thongs weighted with pieces of lead or sharp metal. The victim was stripped to the waist, then bound, in a bent-over position, to a post, and beaten on the bare back with the scourge till the flesh was all torn open. Sometimes death resulted. p. 400, Halley's BIBLE HANDBOOK.

   Jesus' physical agony must have been terrific — but other men have suffered similar deaths. The real meaning of his bruising lies in the fact that his physical wounds were an outward show of the real burden, which was the weight of mankind's iniquities.

3. WHERE DID WE ACQUIRE INIQUITY?
   Iniquities are the sinful habits and traits we have inherited from our forefathers which have been passed down to us through the generations. Exodus 20:5; Psalms 51:5.

4. WHAT ARE SOME OF THESE INIQUITOUS HABITS AND TRAITS?
   Iniquitous habits and traits are such things as the tendency to lie, steal, cheat, gamble, take dope, drink, exaggerate, gossip, hate, covet, lust, to be greedy, jealous, etc.

5. IF INIQUITY IS ONLY THE BREEDING GROUND FOR SIN, WHY MUST I BE FORGIVEN FOR SINS I HAVE NEVER COMMITTED?
   Because God looks at our hearts and knows our inward thoughts and secret desires. Our hearts must be pure before God for it is our hearts that condemn us. Psalms 66:18; 1 Samuel 16:7; Matthew 5:28; 1 John 3:20, 21.

6. CAN WE BE DELIVERED FROM THE CURSE OF INIQUITY?
   Yes! Jesus Christ gave His body to be bruised at Calvary to deliver us from the curse of iniquity. Isaiah 40:2; 53:5; Psalms 103:3; 32:2.

7. HOW MAY I BE DELIVERED FROM THE CURSE OF INIQUITY?
   We can be delivered from the curse of iniquity by sincerely confessing our unrighteousness to Jesus Christ and appropriating to ourselves the work

He did for us on Calvary. Zechariah 13:1; Ezekiel 18:30-32.

8. WHAT ASSURANCE DO I HAVE THAT MY INIQUITY WILL BE TAKEN AWAY?

The deliverance from iniquity is a part of the atonement which Jesus Christ purchased for us at Calvary. If we ask for deliverance from iniquity and believe Him to do it, deliverance is ours. John 14:14; 1 John 1:9; Isaiah 53:11.

9. WILL MY INIQUITIES BE VISITED ON MY CHILDREN AFTER THAT I AM DELIVERED FROM THEM?

No! When God pardons our iniquities, He casts them into the depths of the sea, never to remember them against us and our seed, forever. Micah 7:18, 19; Jeremiah 50:20; Exodus 20:5, 6.

10. TO UNDERSTAND THE POWER OF PRAYER IN BREAKING INIQUITY, READ THE AMAZING STORY OF JABEZ IN 1 CHRONICLES 4:9, 10.

Here we find the story of a young man born in sorrow, surrounded by evil, and officially without pedigree or ancestry in Israel — yet he prayed, and God delivered him from his environment and heredity.

LESSON 2 STUDY QUESTIONS BASED ON "BRUISED FOR OUR INIQUITIES"

1. What is iniquity? How does it differ from sin?
2. What is meant by "bruised for our iniquities"?
3. Where did we acquire iniquity?
4. What are some of these iniquitous habits and traits?
5. If iniquity is only the breeding ground for sin, why must I be forgiven for sins I have never committed?
6. Can we be delivered from the curse of iniquity?
7. How may I be delivered from the curse of iniquity?
8. What assurance do I have that my iniquity will be taken away?
9. Will my iniquities be visited on my children after that I am delivered from them?
10. What light does the story of Jabez shed on the subject of iniquity?

LESSON 3: CHASTISED FOR OUR PEACE

1. **WHY WAS JESUS CHRIST CHASTISED (PUNISHED) FOR OUR PEACE?**
    He took our punishment that we might have peace with God. Colossians 1:20; Ephesians 2:14, 15.

2. **WHAT IS PEACE?**
    Peace, according to the dictionary, is a state of tranquility or quiet — a freedom from all that disturbs or excites. It speaks of order, security, harmony.

3. **WHAT IS PEACE WITH GOD?**
    Peace with God is to be reconciled to God; that is, to be brought back into harmony and friendship with God again.

    "Be ye reconciled to God." 2 Corinthians 5:20. When you are on friendly terms with God, you have peace WITH him, and His peace IN you.

4. **HOW CAN I HAVE PEACE WITH GOD?**
    Peace with God only can be experienced when we come to the Father through His son, Jesus Christ, who is the only mediator between God and man, and receive divine pardon for our sins. Romans 5:1; 8:6; John 14:27; Isaiah 9:6; Romans 6:23.

5. **HOW WILL THIS PEACE AFFECT MY LIFE?**
    This peace from God will . . .

    A. Give us an inner serenity that can come to man through no other means. Philippians 4:7.

    B. Free us from the haunting sense of sin. Hebrews 10:22.

    C. Cleanse us from all feeling of contamination and unfitness. Romans 8:1.

    D. Enable us to stand before God in the hour of our death with this same feeling of peace and security. Psalms 23:4.

    E. Keep our mind sound in the hour of grief, distress or trouble. 2 Timothy 1:7.

6. **HOW CAN I KEEP THIS PEACE?**
    The Lord will keep us in perfect peace if our minds are stayed on Him and we trust in Him to help us in every circumstance of life. Isaiah 26:3.

7. **CAN I HAVE PEACE OF MIND IN THE MIDST OF EVERY TROUBLE?**
    Yes. In the midst of any circumstance of life, we can have the peace that passes all understanding if we appropriate (take to ourselves) the peace that Jesus Christ purchased for us at Calvary.

    "Peace I leave with you, my peace I give unto you: not as the world giveth, give I unto you. Let not your heart be troubled, neither let it be afraid." John 14:27. Note also Hebrews 4:9; Matthew 11:28 and 29.

LESSON 3 STUDY QUESTIONS BASED ON
"CHASTISED FOR OUR PEACE"

1. Why was Jesus Christ chastised (punished) for our peace?
2. What is peace?
3. What is peace with God?
4. How can I have peace with God?
5. How will this peace affect my life?
6. How can I keep this peace?
7. Can I have peace of mind in the midst of every trouble?

LESSON 4: HEALED BY HIS STRIPES

1. WHAT DOES "HEALING" IN ISAIAH 53:5 REFER TO?

   "Healing" in this text refers to the miraculous curing or restoring of a person's physically sick body to a sound or healthy condition.

   This definition is simple and obvious, yet many people are not fully convinced that God can actually heal the human body apart from natural means or medicine.

2. WHAT DOES "WITH HIS STRIPES WE ARE HEALED" MEAN?

   This expression teaches us that God's method of healing the sick is through the beaten, whipped body of the Lord Jesus Christ that bled for us.

3. HOW DO WE KNOW THAT THIS EXPRESSION ACTUALLY REFERS TO JESUS?

   The best way to interpret the Old Testament is to find its fulfillment in the teaching of the New Testament. Isaiah 53 is linked clearly with Matthew 8 – where we find that Jesus' ability to heal people's physical sickness was a direct fulfillment of Isaiah's prophecy.

   Matthew 8:16, 17 – "(he) healed all that were sick: That it might be fulfilled . . . Himself took our infirmities and bare our sicknesses." 1 Peter 2:24 - "by whose stripes ye were healed."

4. THE BIBLE RECORDS 17 BODILY CURES PERFORMED BY THE LORD JESUS CHRIST (He healed MANY more, of course, but these were recorded in the Gospels to give us faith):

   Nobleman's son healed, John 4:46-54.
   Infirm man healed, John 5:1-9.
   Peter's mother-in-law, Matthew 8:14-17; Mark 1:29-31; Luke 4:38, 39.
   A leper, Matthew 8:2-4; Mark 1:40-45; Luke 5:12-15.
   A paralytic, Matthew 9:2-8; Mark 2:3-13; Luke 5:17-26.
   Man with withered hand, Matthew 12:9-14; Mark 3:1-6; Luke 6:6-11.
   Centurion's servant, Matthew 8:5-13; Luke 7:1-10.
   Two blind men, Matthew 9:27-31.
   Deaf and dumb man healed, Mark 7:31-37.
   Blind man at Bethsaida, Mark 8:22-26.
   Blind man in Jerusalem, John 9.
   Woman of 18 years infirmity, Luke 13:10-17.
   Woman with hemorrhage, Matthew 9:20-22; Mark 5:25-34; Luke 8:43-48.
   Man with dropsy, Luke 14:1-6.
   Ten lepers, Luke 17:11-19.
   Blind Bartimaeus, Matthew 20:29-34; Mark 10:46-52; Luke 18:35-43.
   Malchus' ear, Luke 22:50-51.

5. HOW CAN JESUS' BEATING AND DEATH HEAL OUR SICKNESS AND DISEASE?

Jesus Christ carried (bore) sin and the curses of sin (including sickness and disease) in His body to the cross and there destroyed the power of Satan over God's children forever.

Note Isaiah 53:4, 11, 12 where "bear," "borne" and "carried" show that Jesus did more than physically suffer a terrible beating. It was that — but more! As the whip was applied to His body and the precious blood began to flow, His body was made to carry and feel the agony of all mankind's diseases. He became my substitute for my sickness and my sin.

6. CAN EVERYONE BE HEALED?

Yes. If Christ has borne our sickness and redeemed us from the curse, why should we bear it? 1 Peter 2:24; Acts 10:34; Matthew 8:2, 3.

7. WHY, THEN, IS THERE STILL SICKNESS AND DISEASE IN THE WORLD?

There is sickness and disease in the world today for the same reason that there is sin in the world today — people do not know what Jesus Christ has purchased for them. There is forgiveness and deliverance from ALL the power of Satan if we will but receive it, ask for it and partake of it. Redemption is a powerful reality, but to many it is only theory, doctrine or religious formality. Satan has taken advantage of men's ignorance to keep them from the blessing. Hosea 4:6; James 4:2.

8. WHAT IS THAT KNOWLEDGE THAT BRINGS HEALING TO US?

We must know that our bodies have been redeemed from the CURSE of the law for Christ was made a curse for us and has freed us from the power of the devil. Galatians 3:13; 1 Corinthians 6:20.

9. WHAT WAS THE CURSE OF THE LAW?

Physical sickness was a portion of the curse of the law that came upon people because of their disobedience to God's law. Deuteronomy 28:59-61. "Also every sickness and every plague which is not written in the book of the law." Read the entire 28th chapter of Deuteronomy.

10. HOW CAN I BE HEALED?

We receive healing when we exercise faith in the provision Christ made for our healing at Calvary. We must ASK Him in FAITH believing, for this benefit He purchased for us. Matthew 7:7.

11. IS FAITH NECESSARY FOR HEALING?

Yes. Without faith, we receive nothing from God. Hebrews 11:6; Mark 6:5, 6; Matthew 9:29; 22; Luke 7:50.

LESSON 4: HEALED BY HIS STRIPES (Continued)

12. WHAT IS FAITH?

Faith is believing that God will do what He has said in His Word that He will do. In the case of healing, the individual must believe what the Bible says about healing, and then act upon it. Hebrews 11:1; Romans 10:17.

13. HOW IS HEALING ADMINISTERED?

Healing can be administered in five ways:

A. Personal prayer. James 5:16.

B. The sick should call for the elders to come and anoint. James 5:14, 15.

C. The believer's hands can administer healing. Mark 16:17, 18.

D. The spoken Word. Psalms 107:20; Matthew 8:16.

E. Outside helps. Acts 19:11, 12 (cloths); Mark 7:33; 8:23 (spittal).

14. IS THERE ANYTHING THAT CAN PREVENT ME FROM BEING HEALED?

Sin, in its various forms, will separate us from the benefits of God. Unbelief is the most common reason healing is denied. Unconfessed, unforgiven sin and failure to make restitution also can prevent us from receiving from God. Psalms 66:18; Isaiah 59:2; Matthew 6:15; 5:23, 24; Hebrews 11:6; James 1:6, 7; 1 Corinthians 11:30.

15. WHY IS HEALING SOMETIMES DELAYED?

Many times healing is seemingly withheld from us for a time to teach us patience or to give us a greater understanding of God and His ways. When the purpose for which we have been made subject to sickness and disease is accomplished, we are always delivered from our afflictions. 1 Peter 4:19; 5:10; Psalms 103:1-6.

LESSON 4 STUDY QUESTIONS BASED ON
"HEALED BY HIS STRIPES"

1. What does "healing" in Isaiah 53:5 refer to?
2. What does "with His stripes we are healed" mean?
3. How do we know that this expression actually refers to Jesus?
4. Jesus performed some 17 bodily cures in the Gospels. How many of these healings can you remember?
5. How can Jesus' beating and death heal our sickness and disease?
6. Can everyone be healed?
7. Why is there still sickness and disease in the world?
8. What is that knowledge that brings healing to us?
9. What was the curse of the law?

10. How can I be healed?
11. Is faith necessary for healing?
12. What is faith?
13. How is healing administered?
14. Is there anything that can prevent me from being healed?
15. Why is healing sometimes delayed?

PART VII.
THE LIFE AND MINISTRY OF THE HOLY SPIRIT

PART VII. THE LIFE AND MINISTRY OF THE HOLY SPIRIT

PLEASE NOTE:

The lessons in this section of the catechism course could be called: "Steps to Maturity through the Ministry of the Holy Spirit." From simple Salvation to Resurrection Glory, each step in the Christian's walk is accomplished through the Holy Spirit, and is a reproduction of the growth pattern which the Spirit has already shown us in the life of Jesus.

In a way, Part VII is a study of the Christian's experiences in Christ. It is also an analysis of the Holy Spirit and His ministry. Our understanding of the Holy Spirit comes through Bible study, but also through the mysterious and exciting ways in which He deals with us. We understand God the Father through the study of His covenants; we understand Jesus the Son through the study of the Gospels and the work of redemption; we will understand the person of the Holy Spirit as He brings us progressively through the experiences outlined in this part of the catechism.

LESSON 1: THE PERSON OF THE HOLY GHOST

1. WHO IS THE HOLY GHOST?
> The Holy Ghost is true God, a vital part of the Tri-unity of God. He is the out-breathing of God; that is, the life of God·going forth to quicken.

2. WHAT DOES "HOLY GHOST" MEAN?
> "Holy Ghost" means Holy Breath or Holy Spirit. Other terms are used in the Scriptures, such as Spirit of God, Comforter, etc. Various natural things are used also as titles of the Holy Ghost, such as wind, fire, oil and water. Matthew 29:19; Job 33:4; Psalms 33:6; 104:29, 30; Genesis 1:2, 3.

3. IS THE HOLY GHOST AND THE HOLY SPIRIT THE SAME THING?
> Yes. In the original language it is the same word. "Ghost" is simply the Old English way of saying "Spirit." In our teaching, we prefer "Spirit" since it is a more modern, understandable term.

4. WHY DO WE BELIEVE THAT THE HOLY SPIRIT IS TRUE GOD?
> We believe that the Holy Spirit is true God because the Scriptures ascribe to Him:
>
> A. DIVINE NAMES:
>> Acts 5:3, 4   — the Holy Ghost is called "God."
>> 2 Corinthians 3:18 — "of the Lord the Spirit" (center column ref.)
>> 1 Corinthians 3:16 — "God" and "Spirit of God" used synonymously.
>
> B. DIVINE ATTRIBUTES:
>> Hebrews 9:14   — Eternal
>> Psalms 139:7-10   — Omnipresent
>> 1 Corinthians 2:10 — Omniscient
>> Luke 1:35   — Omnipotent
>
> C. DIVINE WORKS:
>> Psalms 33:6   — Creation
>> Romans 8:11   — Impartation of Life
>> John 6:63 and Genesis 2:7
>
> D. DIVINE HONOR AND GLORY:
>> 1 Peter 4:14   — "The Spirit of glory and of God resteth upon you."

5. HIS BASIC CHARACTERISTIC IS TRUTH. John 14:17; 15:26; 16:13.
> All that He does is in conformity to FACT and REALITY. He stays with the facts or to things as they are, and avoids lies, fictions, misrepresentations and the like. Hence, the terrible crime of Ananias and Sapphira — LYING to Him who is TRUTH! Acts 5:3. Note that all that is factual and real is not visible. 2 Corinthians 4:18.

6. HERE ARE SOME OF THE ACTS OF THE HOLY SPIRIT.
   A. He searches the deep things of God for us. 1 Corinthians 2:10.
   B. He speaks to us. Revelation 2:7.
   C. He makes intercession for us. Romans 8:26.
   D. He teaches us. John 14:26.
   E. He leads and guides us. Romans 8:14.
   F. He commissions men for service. Acts 13:2; 20:28.
   G. He glorifies the Lord Jesus Christ. John 16:14; 15:26.

7. WHAT IS THE WORK OF THE HOLY SPIRIT IN RELATION TO THE SCRIPTURES?
   A. He is the author of all Scripture. 2 Peter 1:20, 21.
   B. He is the interpreter of them all. Ephesians 1:17.

8. HOW DOES THE HOLY SPIRIT WORK WITH SINNERS?
   The work of the Holy Spirit in relation to sinners is:

   A. He strives with them. Genesis 6:3.
   B. He witnesses to them. John 15:26.
   C. He convicts or convinces them. John 16:8-11.

9. WHAT TREATMENT HAS THE HOLY SPIRIT RECEIVED OF MEN?

   A. He has been rebelled against and grieved. Isaiah 63:10, R.V.
   B. He is lied to. Acts 5:3.
   C. He is blasphemed. Matthew 12:31.

10. WHAT DOES IT MEAN TO BLASPHEME THE HOLY SPIRIT?
    When a person obstinately attributes to the devil those works which could only be wrought by the Spirit of God, this is blasphemy against the Holy Spirit, i.e., the unpardonable sin. Matthew 12:31 and 32; Mark 3:28-30.

11. WHAT IS THE WORK OF THE HOLY SPIRIT IN RELATION TO JESUS CHRIST?

    A. Christ was conceived by the Holy Spirit. Luke 1:35.
    B. Christ was anointed with the Holy Spirit. Acts 10:38.
    C. Christ was led by the Spirit. Matthew 4:1.
    D. Christ was filled with the Holy Spirit. Luke 4:1.
    E. Christ accomplished His ministry in the power of the Spirit. Luke 4:18, 19.
    F. Christ sacrificially offered Himself through the Spirit. Hebrews 9:14.
    G. Christ was resurrected by the power of the Spirit. Romans 8:11.
    H. Christ's post-resurrection commandments given through the Spirit. Acts 1: 2.
    I. Christ was the bestower of the Holy Spirit. Acts 2:33.

NOTE: The Life of Christ is the perfect example of the Spirit-filled life. His experiences should be duplicated in every Christian's life.

12. WHAT IS THE WORK OF THE HOLY SPIRIT IN RELATION TO BELIEVERS?
We have now given a brief introduction to the Holy Spirit. The remaining lessons in Part VII of the catechism emphasize the vital growth experiences in the life of the child of God that are a product of the Holy Spirit. We might say that these basic experiences are "Steps to Maturity through the Ministry of the Holy Spirit." From simple Salvation to Resurrection Glory, each important step is accomplished through the Holy Spirit and is a reproduction of Jesus' growth pattern. There are other things which we could add in this section, but we feel that it is best at this point to impress each student with the following ways in which he is related to the Holy Spirit.

A. Beginning with Christ through a genuine conversion experience.
B. Baptized into the Lord Jesus Christ through water baptism.
C. The Baptism with the Holy Ghost accompanied by "speaking in tongues."
D. Sanctification of the Spirit that sets us apart for God's service.
E. The Spirit-filled life which produces spiritual fruit and manifestation.
F. The Spirit-filled life which enables us to worship and pray as we ought.
G. The establishment of ministry through Confirmation and the Laying on of Hands.
H. Resurrection Life for our body as the Spirit's climax!

LESSON 1 STUDY QUESTIONS BASED ON "THE PERSON OF THE HOLY GHOST"

1. Who is the Holy Ghost?
2. What does "Holy Ghost" mean?
3. Is the Holy Ghost and the Holy Spirit the same thing?
4. Why do we believe that the Holy Spirit is true God?
5. What is the basic characteristic of the Holy Spirit?
6. What are some of the acts of the Holy Spirit?
7. What is the work of the Holy Spirit in relation to the scriptures?
8. How does the Holy Spirit work with sinners?
9. What treatment has the Holy Spirit received of men?
10. What does it mean to blaspheme the Holy Spirit?
11. What is the work of the Holy Spirit in relation to Jesus Christ?
12. What is the work of the Holy Spirit in relation to believers?

LESSON 2: BEGINNING WITH CHRIST

1. HOW DOES A PERSON BEGIN THE CHRISTIAN LIFE?

   The purpose of this lesson is to outline in simple terms the first important step in the Christian life. A person's first step is gaining ASSURANCE that he has really become a Child of God. Note "know" in 1 John 2:3, 21; 3:5, 6, 14, 24; 5:18, 19, 20. The remainder of this lesson will elaborate on what happens and how this wonderful assurance comes to the human heart.

2. WHAT TERMS DESCRIBE THE FIRST STEP OF BEGINNING WITH CHRIST?

   There are various ways of describing the same experience of becoming a Christian or beginning with Christ. Here are some: "saved," "converted," "born again," "transformed," "regenerated," "justified by faith," "new creature," "accept Jesus Christ as your own personal Saviour," etc.

3. WHY ARE THERE SO MANY WAYS OF DESCRIBING THE SAME EVENT?

   When a sinner becomes a saint, the experience is so great that it cannot be adequately described by just one expression.

4. HOW DID JESUS DESCRIBE THIS BEGINNING EXPERIENCE OF SALVATION?

   Jesus used a variety of expressions and illustrations. John's Gospel illustrates this: 1:12, "received Him"; 2:23, "believed in His Name"; 3:3, "be born again"; 4:14, "Whosoever drinketh of the water"; 5:40, "Come to me"; 6:51, "If any man eat of this bread"; etc., each chapter adding some new thought.

5. WHAT IS A MAN'S CONDITION BEFORE HE BEGINS THE CHRISTIAN LIFE?

   The Bible calls all non-Christians "sinners," which means that they transgress (or willfully break) God's law. 1 John 3:4. The sinner is plagued by two kinds of sin:

   A. Original Sin. This refers to the total corruption of man's whole human nature. It means that man, by nature, is without true fear, love and trust in God. He is without righteousness, is inclined only to evil and is spiritually blind, dead and an enemy of God. Genesis 8:23; Romans 7:18; 8:7; 1 Corinthians 2:14; Ephesians 2:1; 4:22; Psalms 51:5; John 3:6.

   B. Actual Sin. Actual sin is EVERY ACT against a commandment of God in thoughts, desires, words or deed. Matthew 15:19; James 1:15; 4:17. It is the original sin in our lives that causes us to commit all manner of actual sins. Matthew 7:17.

6. WHAT IS THE BIG PROBLEM THAT EVERY SINNER MUST FACE IF HE IS TO BECOME A CHRISTIAN?

   Because God is holy and righteous, He cannot tolerate sin. Therefore, every

126

sinner must get rid of his sins if he is to find fellowship with God. The sinner finds salvation from sin ONLY in the Gospel, which tells us that Christ, as our substitute fulfilled the Law and suffered and died for us. John 8:21, 24, 34.

7. **WHAT DOES THE GOSPEL INSTRUCT US TO DO TO FIND SALVATION?**
The Gospel instructs me to confess and to repent of my sins (actual) to Christ in faith, believing that He will forgive my sins and cleanse me from all unrighteousness. 1 John 1:9.

Note: Original sin, or the nature of sin, only can be remitted through the cleansing of the blood of Christ and water baptism (note next lesson).

8. **HOW DO WE RECEIVE FAITH TO BELIEVE IN CHRIST'S WORK OF REDEMPTION?**
By hearing of the Gospel, the Holy Spirit brings me to faith in Christ by imparting to me the knowledge of the redemption Jesus Christ purchased for me at Calvary. John 5:24; Romans 10:9, 10; Hosea 4:6; 1 Corinthians 2:12, 14.

9. **WHY IS IT NECESSARY THAT THE HOLY GHOST WORK THIS FAITH IN US?**
According to the Scriptures, I am by nature spiritually blind, dead, an enemy of God; therefore, I cannot by my own reason or strength, believe in Jesus Christ, or come to Him. 1 Corinthians 2:14; 12:3; Romans 8:7; Ephesians 2:1, 8, 9.

10. **WHAT HAS THE HOLY GHOST DONE TO BRING US TO CHRIST?**
The Holy Ghost has called us by the Gospel, that is, He has invited us to partake of Christ's blessings which are offered to us in the Gospel. 2 Thessalonians 2:14; 2 Timothy 1:9; Revelation 22:17.

11. **WHAT DOES THE HOLY GHOST WORK IN US WHEN HE CALLS US BY THE GOSPEL?**
The Holy Ghost works faith in me, through the Gospel by:

A. Convicting me of my sin. John 16:8; Acts 2:37.

B. Showing me that I am in a lost state and under condemnation. John 16:8; Acts 11:21.

C. Giving me the desire to have my sins pardoned when I have been shown the greatness of my sinful state. Luke 18:13; Romans 3:23.

D. Granting me repentance for my sins. Acts 11:18; Romans 2:4; Hebrews 12:17. Note: Repentance is a gift from God.

E. Giving me faith to believe that if I confess my sins (actual) and forsake my sins, Christ will forgive my sins and give me right standing with God, the Father. 1 John 1:9; Proverbs 28:13; Isaiah 55:7; Ephesians 2:8, 9; Acts 16:31.

12. WHAT IS THIS SAVING WORK OF THE HOLY SPIRIT CALLED?

This work of the Holy Spirit is called justification. Romans 3:24, 28; 5:1, 2, 9.

13. WHAT IS JUSTIFICATION?

Justification is the "right standing" with God which I receive when I believe Jesus Christ shed His blood for my sin (actual) and appropriate the benefits of the Cross to myself. 2 Corinthians 5:19, 21; Romans 4:5; 8:33.

To be JUSTIFIED means that I stand before God washed from my sins; I stand before God as though I had never sinned.

14. WHY MUST WE EVER FIRMLY MAINTAIN THE DOCTRINE OF JUSTIFICATION BY GRACE, FOR CHRIST'S SAKE, THROUGH FAITH?

A. Because it is a foundational doctrine of the Christian religion. Acts 4:12; 10:43.

B. Because it distinguishes the Christian religion from false religions, all of which teach salvation by works. Galatians 5:4, 5.

C. Because this doctrine gives enduring comfort to penitent sinners. Acts 16:30, 31, 34.

D. Because the doctrine gives all glory to God. Revelation 1:5, 6.

E. Because it is the means by which we are led into the full knowledge of redemption through Jesus Christ. Hosea 6:3; Romans 8:29, 30.

LESSON 2 STUDY QUESTIONS BASED ON "BEGINNING WITH CHRIST"

1. How does a person begin the Christian life?
2. What terms describe this first step of beginning with Christ?
3. Why are there so many ways of describing the same event?
4. How did Jesus describe this beginning experience of salvation?
5. What is a man's condition before he begins the Christian life?
6. What is the big problem that every sinner must face if he is to become a Christian?
7. What does the Gospel instruct us to do to find salvation?
8. How do we receive faith to believe in Christ's work of redemption?
9. Why is it necessary that the Holy Ghost work this faith in us?

10. What has the Holy Ghost done to bring us to Christ?
11. What does the Holy Ghost work in us when he calls us by the Gospel?
12. What is the saving work of the Holy Spirit called?
13. What is justification?
14. Why must we ever firmly maintain the doctrine of justification by grace, for Christ's sake, through faith?

LESSON 3: BAPTIZED INTO CHRIST, A STUDY OF NEW TESTAMENT WATER BAPTISM

1. WHAT IS WATER BAPTISM?

    Baptism is a holy sacrament (religious ceremony) commanded by Christ. Outwardly, a person is submerged completely under water in the Name of the Lord Jesus Christ. Inwardly, a person undergoes a spiritual work of grace which is DEATH UNTO SIN and a NEW BIRTH UNTO RIGHTEOUSNESS. 1 Peter 3:21, Amp.

2. WHAT DOES THE WORD "BAPTISM" MEAN?

    The Greek word translated as "baptism" actually means to immerse or dip. It means to "whelm," that is, cover wholly with fluid. The Bible shows Baptism to be more than "sprinkling"; for instance: Matthew 3:16; Mark 1:9, 10; John 3:23; Acts 8:38.

    Thus we see that Jesus and His followers went INTO the water and then came up OUT OF the water — giving us a clear pattern to follow.

3. WHO CAN BE BAPTIZED?

    Anyone who has genuinely repented of his sin and has been justified by faith in the Lord Jesus Christ (see previous lesson) can and should be baptized. Mark 16:16; Acts 2:38.

4. SHOULD BABIES BE BAPTIZED?

    No. The Bible teaches that only people old enough to repent and believe should be baptized. A parent's good intentions are not enough. We must individually decide.

5. WHO SHOULD DO THE BAPTIZING?

    Spirit-filled ministers of the Gospel of Christ should baptize the new converts. Such a minister should have an authority that has proven itself before the Church and the world. The authority and significance of the baptism is reflected in the caliber of the ministry.

6. SHOULD A PERSON BE RE-BAPTIZED?

    If you were not a Christian when you were baptized, you certainly should! Acts 19:4, 5 shows that a dead ritual is not sufficient. Also, if in your heart you do not feel that your water baptism was an actual fulfillment of the things taught in the Scripture, you should be properly baptized.

7. WHEN A PERSON IS BAPTIZED, 3 THINGS ARE SIGNIFIED OUTWARDLY:

    A. Farewell to Heathenism. It means the severing of relations with the ungodly ways of heathenism. It signifies the start of the CHRISTian life and dedication to Christ and the work of His Church. Baptism into His name passes the ownership of our life over to the Lord Jesus Christ.

  B. A New Standard of Living. From this point on, the Christian is to live according to the New Covenant of the Lord Jesus Christ. This entails both its blessings and its obligations.

  C. A Disciple of Jesus. This means being a follower, a student and a witness to others of all that Jesus stands for.

8. WHAT IS THE INWARD WORK THAT IS ACCOMPLISHED IN WATER BAPTISM?

There are various ways of describing the spiritual experience that occurs in water baptism. Here are six expressions that should be meaningful to every believer:

  A. Baptism in the Name of the Lord Jesus Christ.

  B. The Remission of Sins, Acts 2:38.

  C. The New Birth, John 3:3-7.

  D. Circumcision of the Heart, Colossians 2:11, 12; 2 Corinthians 5:17.

  E. Burial of the Old Man, Romans 6:3-11.

  F. Baptized into His Body, 1 Corinthians 12:13.

9. NOTE THESE REFERENCES ON WATER BAPTISM:

Matthew 28:19; Mark 16:15, 16; Acts 2:38, 41; 8:12, 36, 38; 9:18; 10:47, 48; 16:14, 15, 33; 18:8; 19:5; 22:16.

10. WHAT IS THE INTERPRETATION FOR THE EXPRESSION FOUND IN MATTHEW 28:19: "IN THE NAME OF THE FATHER, AND OF THE SON, AND OF THE HOLY GHOST"?

  A. THE SIGNIFICANCE OF GOD'S NAME. Devout men of every age have hungered to know the Name of the true and living God. In Eastern Lands a man's name and personality are synonymous and this is especially true in the Bible concept of God. GOD AND HIS NAME ARE ONE; therefore, His Name must be a self-expression of all that He is. The word "God" is not a name, but rather a simple title of Diety. There are many "gods" among the heathen; however, according to the Bible, there is only ONE true GOD. 1 Corinthians 8:5; Galatians 4:8. The ONE God of the Bible that reveals Himself as Father, Son and Holy Spirit has a three-fold Name of rich spiritual significance. Note again on page 40: "Lesson 4: What is the Name of God?"

  B. WHAT IS THE NAME OF THE FATHER? Exodus 3:13 and 14 is the basis for understanding the Father's Name. The original Hebrew word used meant "I AM" — an expression which conveyed the undying, ever-present nature of the true God. This original word was so sacred that the Jews did not pronounce it but rather used a substituted word in its place — "Adonai" which means "Lord." Every time you see the capitalized "L-O-R-D" in the King James Old Testament, it means that the original Name of God is in the Hebrew text. It can be clearly seen, therefore, that the expressed Name of God the Father was "THE LORD"; to confirm this thought, we have the witness of Jesus, the early Church, the Jewish Rabbis, Israel throughout the Old Testament and the present Jewish Old Testament Scriptures.

C. WHAT IS THE NAME OF THE SON? "Thou shalt call His Name JESUS," Luke 1:26-31; Matthew 1:21; Luke 2:21. Note also Proverbs 30:4; Isaiah 7:14; 9:6-7.

D. WHAT IS THE NAME OF THE HOLY GHOST? The Name, CHRIST, means the ANOINTED and it has pleased God that this significant Name should be associated with the Holy Spirit. JESUS became the CHRIST, or the anointed one, when God's Spirit came upon Him in the Jordan. Note Acts 10:38.

E. OUR SIMPLE CONCLUSION, THEREFORE, is that the Name of the Father ("LORD") and the Name of the Son ("JESUS") and the Name of the Holy Ghost ("CHRIST") are fulfilled in the Name of "THE LORD JESUS CHRIST"!

This is why Peter told the Jews that "God hath made that same JESUS, whom ye have crucified, both LORD and CHRIST." Acts 2:36. Peter then tells them to be baptized in the "Name of the Lord Jesus Christ." He did not say "Father, Son and Holy Ghost" because he fulfilled the meaning of Jesus' commandment when he actually used the literal names as they applied to the son of God, in whom dwelleth the fulness of the Godhead. Colossians 2:9.

THESE FIVE READINGS contain the only record in the Acts of the baptismal "Name" commanded to be, or stated to have been, used in baptisms:

A. Acts 2:38   —   "in the name of Jesus Christ"
B. Acts 8:16   —   "in the name of the Lord Jesus"
C. Acts 10:48 —   "in the name of the Lord"
D. Acts 19:5   —   "in the name of the Lord Jesus"
E. Acts 22:16 —   "calling on the name of the Lord"

It is interesting to notice that the King James Version, the Revised Version, the Catholic Version, etc., are not all in harmony on the exact names to be used in each of these Scriptures. It is wonderful to note, however, that most of the older manuscripts tend to hold to the full name of "The Lord Jesus Christ."

Baptism performed "IN the Name" puts "The Name" UPON the one so baptized; and those who have had "The Name" put upon them in baptism are declared to have been baptized "INTO the Name," because they have in Baptism so "PUT ON" or "BEEN CLOTHED WITH" The Name. Check these references: Romans 6:3; 13:14; 2 Corinthians 5:17; Galatians 3:27; Ephesians 4:24; Colossians 3:9.

11. THE WORK OF THE HOLY SPIRIT IN WATER BAPTISM.
Many people go down into the waters of baptism dry and come up wet — and that is the extent of their experience. This is tragic!

Experience has shown that new converts need to be instructed about water baptism. If there is a group of converts that need baptism, it would be wise to have a class of instruction for them. Have each candidate thoroughly aware of the Bible's teaching on the subject. Above all, each candidate must be challenged to believe that God's Spirit will work within his heart in a very special way.

We must be convinced of the work of the Holy Spirit in water baptism. As the candidate is lowered into the water, a tremendous work of God should take place!

The candidate steps out of the life of heathenism into Christ and His New Covenant. The heart is circumcised, the old nature is buried, the Name of the Lord Jesus Christ enfolds the candidate, there is a remission of sins that conquers the iniquitous nature. In a full sense of the word, the candidate comes out of the water in "newness of life" energized by the Holy Spirit. If the candidate has not received the Baptism with the Holy Ghost, hands should be laid upon him at this time and opportunity given for this Divine expression. It should not be uncommon for people to come up out of the water speaking in tongues!

LESSON 3 STUDY QUESTIONS BASED ON
"BAPTIZED INTO CHRIST THROUGH WATER BAPTISM"

1. What is water baptism?
2. What does the word "baptism" mean?
3. Who can be baptized?
4. Should babies be baptized?
5. Who should do the baptizing?
6. Should a person be re-baptized?

7. When a person is baptized, what 3 things are signified outwardly?
8. What is the inward work that is accomplished in water baptism?
9. List some of the key references on water baptism.
10. What is the interpretation for the expression found in Matthew 28:19: "In the Name of the Father, and of the Son and of the Holy Ghost"?
11. What is the work of the Holy Spirit in water baptism?

LESSON 4: THE BAPTISM WITH THE HOLY GHOST

Isaiah prophesied it, Joel verified it, John preached it, Jesus promised it, I have it, and Peter said that it's for as many as God shall call — praise the Lord!

1. **IF A PERSON HAS BEEN SAVED AND BAPTIZED IN WATER, IS THERE ANY OTHER EXPERIENCE NECESSARY?**
    Yes indeed! Many of God's great revelations are three-fold, and the beginning experiences of Christianity are no exception. Every one should have these three experiences to properly begin their Christian walk: [1] Salvation, [2] Water Baptism, [3] Baptism with the Holy Ghost.

2. **DOES THIS MEAN THAT THE NEW CONVERT DOES NOT HAVE THE SPIRIT?**
    The new convert is saved or born again through the Holy Spirit, but there is yet another work of the Spirit to be done in his life.

3. **WHERE IN THE BIBLE DOES IT SHOW THAT THERE IS AN EXPERIENCE WITH THE HOLY SPIRIT THAT IS ENTIRELY SEPARATE FROM SALVATION AND WATER BAPTISM?**
    Read the remarkable story in Acts 8. Here we find a revival of such magnitiude that people have been converted, baptized in water, healed, delivered of demons and made joyful (vss. 5-8, 12). Yet, they still needed to "receive the Holy Ghost" (15-17).

4. **WHAT IS THIS EXPERIENCE CALLED?**
    This third vital step in the Christian walk is called "The Baptism with the Holy Ghost." Matthew 3:11; Mark 1:8; Luke 3:16; Acts 1:5; 11:16; John 1:33.

5. **WHAT IS THE BAPTISM WITH THE HOLY GHOST?**
    The baptism with the Holy Ghost is a baptism of the believer into the Holy Spirit, at which time he is given entrance into the realm of unlimited, measureless power to do the works of Christ. Acts 1:8.

6. **HOW DOES THE BAPTISM WITH THE HOLY GHOST AFFECT THE BELIEVER'S LIFE?**
    A. AUTHORITY to witness and minister to others. Acts 1:8; Mark 16:17, 18.

    B. INSPIRATION for true worship. John 4:24; Philippians 3:3; Hebrews 2:12.

    C. POWER in Prayer. Romans 8:26; 1 Corinthians 14:15; Jude 20; Ephesians 6:18.

    D. UNDERSTANDING of the Scripture. 1 John 2:20, 27; 1 Corinthians 2:12; John 16:13-15.

E.   GUIDANCE from God's Voice. Acts 13:2; Mark 13:11.

F.   MANIFESTATIONS of the Spirit. 1 Corinthians 12 and 14.

G.   THE FRUIT AND GRACES of the Holy Spirit. Galatians 5:16-23, 25.

7. WHAT MUST WE DO TO RECEIVE THE GIFT OF THE HOLY GHOST?
We receive the Holy Ghost by asking God for it after that we have obeyed His word, i.e., "Repent and be baptized every one of you in the name of Jesus Christ for the remission of sins, and ye shall receive the gift of the Holy Ghost." Acts 2:38; Luke 11:13.

8. HOW MAY I RECEIVE THE GIFT OF THE HOLY GHOST?
The Lord employs two distinct methods of baptizing believers in the Holy Spirit;

A.   By the sovereign act of God. As, Acts 2:2-4; 10:44-46.
B.   By impartation by the laying on of hands. Acts 8:14-19.

9. HOW DO YOU KNOW WHEN YOU HAVE RECEIVED THE HOLY GHOST?
It is more than just "taking it by faith." God gives a tangible supernatural sign in your own body — your tongue speaks a language you have never learned. This is called "speaking in tongues" or glossalalia.

10. DOES THE BIBLE TEACH THAT YOU MUST SPEAK IN TONGUES TO HAVE THE SPIRIT?
The Bible does not say that you MUST speak in tongues to have the baptism, but it does teach us by illustration that if you have the baptism with the Holy Ghost, you will be given the immediate evidence of speaking in tongues.

11. FOUR CLASSIC EXAMPLES OF THE SPIRIT BAPTISM ARE LISTED IN THE ACTS:
The Lord uses these four different groups to show that no ethnic or social group was excluded from this great experience.

A.   THE JEWS, Chapter 2 — spoke in tongues.

B.   THE SAMARITANS, Chapter 8 — by inference, speaking in tongues, for every other manifestation had already occurred in the revival.

C.   THE ROMANS, Chapter 10 — spoke in tongues.

D.   THE GREEK HEATHEN, Chapter 19 — spoke in tongues and prophesied.

12. IS THIS DOCTRINE OF TONGUES TAUGHT SOMEWHERE ELSE IN THE BIBLE?
Tongues is also mentioned in 1 Corinthians 12, 13 and 14, but only in doctrinal explanation of the Spirit's activity AFTER the baptism. The Acts

is the historical record and was inspired by God to be our example of the initial experience.

13. WHY DOES GOD CHOOSE THIS PECULIAR MANIFESTATION TO PROVE THE BAPTISM?

The tongue is our body's most unruly member (James 3), and yet it is the way whereby the heart finds expression (Matthew 12:34). Tongues indicates that the Spirit has possessed both the inner man as well as the outer man.

14. WHO CAN RECEIVE THIS EXPERIENCE?

Every believer in Christ is a candidate. Acts 2:39.

15. WHAT INSTRUCTION SHOULD BE FOLLOWED TO RECEIVE THE GIFT OF THE HOLY GHOST?

Here is a suggested course:

A. Pray to Jesus Christ for the gift of the Holy Ghost. Acts 8:14; Luke 11:13.

B. Enter into the presence of the Lord with praise and thanksgiving knowing He has heard our request and will grant us our petition. Psalms 100:4; 134:2; Luke 24:52, 53.

C. A person should worship and praise God. Then as he becomes aware of the presence of the Holy Spirit, a deeper praise wells up in the heart. Then he should open his mouth and drink in the Spirit of God. John 4:10, 13, 14; Job 29:23.

D. While drinking in the Spirit of God, anointed hands should be laid upon the candidate and the gift of the Holy Ghost imparted to him. Acts 8:17-19.

E. As he continues to drink in the Spirit, the organs of speech are quickened, producing the stammering of lips. Isaiah 28:11; 1 Corinthians 14:21.

F. As the Holy Spirit takes over our thoughts, we become aware of words foreign to our understanding. We should yield our most unruly member the tongue, to speak the words introduced by the Holy Spirit.

In yielding our organs of speech to Him, we are baptized (or immersed) into the Holy Spirit, entering a realm heretofore foreign to us. Acts 2:4 (Weymouth): "the Spirit gave them words to utter."

137

LESSON 4 STUDY QUESTIONS BASED ON
"THE BAPTISM WITH THE HOLY GHOST"

1. If a person has been saved and baptized in water, is there any other experience necessary?
2. Does this mean that the new convert does not have the Spirit?
3. Where in the Bible does it show that there is an experience with the Holy Spirit that is entirely separate from salvation and water baptism?
4. What is this experience called?
5. What is the baptism with the Holy Ghost?
6. How does the baptism with the Holy Ghost affect the believer's life?
7. What must we do to receive the gift of the Holy Ghost?
8. How may I receive the gift of the Holy Ghost?
9. How do you know when you have received the Holy Ghost.
10. Does the Bible teach that you must speak in tongues to have the Spirit?
11. What are four classic examples of the Spirit baptism listed in Acts?
12. Is this doctrine of tongues taught somewhere else in the Bible?
13. Why does God choose this peculiar manifestation to prove the baptism?
14. Who can receive this experience?
15. What instruction should be followed to receive the gift of the Holy Ghost?

LESSON 5: SANCTIFIED LIVING, A STUDY OF THE DOCTRINE OF SANCTI-FICATION

1. **WHAT IS SANCTIFICATION?**

   Sanctification is that working of the Holy Spirit that SETS US APART for God's service. It means that a person's life has been consecrated in such a way to God that it is appropriate for God's use. Romans 12:1.

2. **WHY MUST WE BE SANCTIFIED?**

   We must be sanctified if we expect to be used of God. God's great delight is to use men, women and vessels that are set apart for His service alone. 2 Corinthians 6:17; Galatians 1:15, 16; Hebrews 11:16.

3. **WHAT DOES IT MEAN TO BE "SET APART" TO GOD ALONE?**

   Real consecration means that our affections and our interests are undivided and unwavering. We literally present our bodies and our minds as living sacrifices unto Him. Romans 12:1, 2; 1 Thessalonians 5:23; James 4:8-10 (read in Amplified New Testament).

4. **HOW CAN THIS STATE OF SANCTIFICATION BE MORE FULLY DES-CRIBED?**

   Santification is the complete dedication of our lives, time, talents and possessions for His kingdom. Luke 14:26, 27; 9:23; Mark 8:34; 10:17-27; Matthew 16:24.

5. **WHEN DOES SANCTIFICATION TAKE PLACE IN THE BELIEVER'S LIFE?**

   A. Sanctification begins with the consecration of the will and continues throughout our walk with God in every phase of life. 1 Peter 3:15.

   B. Sanctification is both instantaneous and continual — instantaneous as we are shown our need for sanctification and as we yield to God; continual as we progress in God and continue to yeild. Romans 12:2; Ephesians 5:26, 27.

   NOTE: Sanctification represents a growth IN holiness, rather than INTO holiness out of something else. It doesn't all happen at once, but rather is a progressive work of the Holy Spirit as we grow in our understanding of God's will.

6. **WHAT PRODUCES THIS WORK OF SANCTIFICATION?**

   Eight things are mentioned in the New Testament that produce sanctification in the Christian's life:

   A. GOD THE FATHER: Jude 1; 1 Thessalonians 5:23.

   B. THE BLOOD AND SACRIFICE OF CHRIST: Hebrews 9:14; 10:10, 14, 29; 13:12.

139

    C.   THE HOLY SPIRIT: Romans 15:16; 1 Corinthians 6:11; 2 Thessalonians 2:13; 1 Peter 1:2.

    D.   THE WORD OF GOD: John 17:17, 19; Acts 20:32; Ephesians 5:26; 1 Timothy 4:5; 2 Peter 1:2.

    E.   A SAVED HUSBAND OR WIFE: 1 Corinthians 7:14.

    F.   PERSONAL EFFORT: 1 Thessalonians 4:3; 2 Timothy 2:21; 1 Peter 3:15.

    G.   FAITH: Acts 26:17.

    H.   PRAYER: 1 Timothy 4:5.

7.   HOW CAN WE RECEIVE THIS WORK OF SANCTIFICATION?
Our basic attitude and will must be affected by the Holy Spirit so that:

    A.   We realize that our own will is contrary to the will of God. Romans 8:7.

    B.   We realize that our self-will has no place in the Kingdom of God. Matthew 6:10.

    C.   We desire to have our will brought under subjection to the will of God. Psalms 143:10; Hebrews 10:9.

    D.   We are granted repentance for our willfulness. Proverbs 12:15; 13:15; 14:12.

    E.   We are given strength and power to perform His will. Psalms 37:5.

8.   WHAT WILL SANCTIFICATION DO FOR US?
Sanctification will give us inward peace and confidence that we are walking in the will of God. Isaiah 30:15; Psalms 16:11; Hebrews 10:35; Romans 8:6.

9.   HOW WILL SANCTIFICATION AFFECT OUR DAILY LIVES?
Sanctification will cause us to live by the principles of God's Kingdom rather than by the principles of the world. Whereas, we once lived for ourselves; now we live for others. Whereas, we once grasped for gain; now we give ourselves and our substance to God. John 17:17; Matthew 6:33.

10.   WHAT IS THE POSITION OF THE SANCTIFIED CHRISTIAN?
We are one with Christ. He is our head and we are His body. Ephesians 5:30; 1 Corinthians 1:2, 30; Colossians 2:6-10; Hebrews 2:11; Jude 1.

11.   WHAT IS THE "LAW OF SIN"?
The Law of Sin is:

    A.   An inescapable force that is at work in our bodies from the time of birth which works to the ultimate destruction of our flesh — the death of the human body. Psalms 103:14-16; Hebrews 9:27.

    B.   The enemy of the Spirit of God that wars against the inner man. Romans 8:7; 7:22-25.

12. WHAT IS THE PURPOSE FOR THE LAW OF SIN?

The purpose for the law of sin is to prove to us the sufficiency of the grace of God. Without the law of sin, we never would see our need for God or would we be able to fight the good fight of faith that makes us true soldiers of the cross. 2 Corinthians 12:9; 1 Corinthians 10:13; 2 Peter 2:9.

13. HOW CAN WE OVERCOME THE LAW OF SIN?

The only way we can overcome the Law of Sin is by being sanctified and by putting on the whole armour of God so that we can withstand the temptations of the law of sin. Romans 13:12-14; 2 Corinthians 10:3-5.

14. IS IT POSSIBLE TO BE DELIVERED FROM THE LAW OF SIN?

It will happen, but we cannot be delivered from the Law of Sin as long as we are in this mortal body of flesh. God has put this law into our bodies in order to perfect the soul by temptation. At the coming of our Lord and Saviour Jesus Christ, this body will be laid aside and the Law of Sin will be laid aside with it. Then we shall be clothed with a new house from Heaven and have sinless perfection. 1 Corinthians 15:51-53.

15. WHAT IS THE REWARD OF THE FAITHFUL?

The reward of the faithful who resist the Law of Sin in their bodies is power from God to make them effectual witnesses, a crown of life and life everlasting with our Lord in His Kingdom. Romans 8:18; Philippians 3:14; 2 Timothy 4:7, 8.

LESSON 5 STUDY QUESTIONS BASED ON "SANCTIFIED LIVING"

1.   What is sanctification?
2.   Why must we be sanctified?
3.   What does it mean to be "set apart" to God alone?
4.   How can this state of sanctification be more fully described?
5.   When does sanctification take place in the believer's life?
6.   What produces this work of sanctification?
7.   How can we receive this work of sanctification?
8.   What will sanctification do for us?

9. How will sanctification affect our daily lives?
10. What is the position of the sanctified Christian?
11. What is the "Law of Sin"?
12. What is the purpose for the law of sin?
13. How can we overcome the law of sin?
14. Is it possible to be delivered from the law of sin?
15. What is the reward of the faithful?

LESSON 6: THE SPIRIT-FILLED LIFE – FRUIT AND MANIFESTATIONS

1. **WHAT IS "THE SPIRIT-FILLED LIFE"?**
   After the Christian has been baptized with the Holy Ghost, he then should live according to the direction of the Spirit of God. A Spirit-filled life is one that is controlled and motivated by the Holy Spirit. Romans 8:1, 4, 12, 14.

   "But I say, walk and live habitually in the Holy Spirit – responsive to and controlled and guided by the Spirit; then you will certainly not gratify the cravings and desires of the flesh – of human nature without God." Galatians 5:16, Amplified New Testament.

2. **HOW DOES THE SPIRIT-FILLED LIFE FIND EXPRESSION?**
   In this course we will deal with four major ways in which the Spirit of God expresses Himself in and through the Christian. This lesson will emphasize the Fruit of the Spirit and the Manifestations of the Spirit. The next lesson will cover Prayer and Worship in the Spirit-filled believer's life.

3. **WHAT IS MEANT BY "THE FRUIT OF THE SPIRIT"?**
   This expression is found in Galatians 5:22 and refers to the very nature of the Holy Spirit that is worked in and through the Christian. Fruit is something that is grown, not created instantly. It should be noted that fruit is the sure sign of healthy life in a tree. Even older people can expect to continue bearing Spiritual fruit. Psalms 92:14.

4. **WHY DOES IT SAY FRUIT, RATHER THAN FRUITS?**
   Paul speaks here not of fruits (various kinds) but of fruit (one kind). A lovely nine-fold cluster of fruit is described here and brings to remembrance Jesus' teaching on fruit in John 15:1-8, 16. Compare Philippians 1:11 – "Fruit of righteousness" (singular in Greek). Ephesians 5:9 – "Fruit of the Light" (R.V., Amp. New Testament and others).

5. **HOW CAN WE PRODUCE THE FRUIT OF THE SPIRIT?**
   Someone has said that "It is not so much what we do FOR Christ that counts as much as what we do IN CHRIST." Paul shows us that the works of the flesh involve hard, grinding, fruitless toil, which yields in the end the wages of death. Fleshly endeavor, even when it is FOR Christ, cannot yield the fruit of the Spirit that comes by simply allowing the Spirit to move in and through us – like the sap of life in the vine bringing fruitfulness into the branches. We can affect the environment (just as a tree can be cultivated and pruned), but it is the Life within that brings forth the fruit.

6. **HERE IS THE NINE-FOLD FRUIT OF THE SPIRIT THAT CHRIST DESIRES TO PRODUCE IN AND THROUGH US.**
   Additional definitions will help clarify.

143

A. LOVE — 1 Corinthians 13.

B. JOY — Gladness (A). "In the Lord" (Philippians 4:4), not through circumstances.

C. PEACE — Of God, which guards the believing heart (Philippians 4:7).

D. LONGSUFFERING — Patience (A, W.), an even temper (A, B.), for-bearance (A, W.), despite injuries or wrongs.

E. GENTLENESS — Kindness (A, B, W, WM, RV); kindly disposition toward others.

F. GOODNESS — Benevolence (A, WM); active beneficence (NBC). Note the life of Barnabas, Acts 11:24.

G. FAITH — Faithfulness (A, W); fidelity (B), as Titus 2:10; good faith (W).

H. MEEKNESS — Humility, gentleness (A, B, W); not standing on one's rights (NBC). Matthew 5:5; 11:29; 2 Corinthians 10:1.

I. TEMPERANCE — Self-control (RV, W, B), self-restraint (WM, A), continence (A); keeping firm hand on desires and passions. 2 Peter 1:6.

NOTE: A (Amplified New Testament), B (Berkeley Version), W (Williams) WM (Weymouth), RV (Revised Version), NBC (New Bible Commentary).

7. WHAT ARE THE GIFTS OR MANIFESTATIONS OF THE SPIRIT?
The nine gifts or manifestations of the Spirit mentioned in 1 Corinthians 12:8-10 are supernatural demonstrations of Divine ability.

Just as a man's activities are in the realm of either the mental, the physical or communication, so the Body of Christ (The Church) must learn to function within these three categories of manifestation:

A. REVELATION — Word of wisdom, Knowledge and Discerning of Spirits.

B. POWER — faith, healing and miracles.

C. UTTERANCE — prophecy, tongues and interpretation of tongues.

8. HOW MAY WE RECEIVE SPIRITUAL GIFTS?
Spiritual gifts may be received in different ways:

A. A manifestation of the Spirit may become evident following the receiving of the gift of the Holy Ghost. Acts 19:6; 3:6; 1 Corinthians 12:8-11.

B. Spiritual gifts are imparted by the laying on of the hands of the presbytery with prophecy. 1 Timothy 4:14.

C. Spiritual gifts are given in answer to fervent prayer, rising out of an evident spiritual need. 1 Corinthians 12:31.

9. CAN A PERSON MERIT A SPIRITUAL MANIFESTATION OR GIFT?

We cannot merit spiritual gifts; they are gifts of Christ to born-again, Spirit-filled believers because they are members of the Body of Christ. Every member must have a function, a place to fill, a duty to perform, when they come together comprising the complete expression of Christ, the fulness of God. 1 Corinthians 12:1, 4-7, 2 Timothy 1:6; 1 Timothy 1:18.

10. WHY MUST EACH MEMBER KNOW HIS PLACE IN THE BODY OF CHRIST?

Unless each member knows his place in the Body of Christ, he cannot be of full value to God and the Church. Ephesians 1:18.

11. IS IT NECESSARY TO HAVE THE GIFTS OF THE SPIRIT OPERATIVE IN THE CHURCH?

Yes. Unless the gifts of the Spirit are operative in the Church, the Body of Christ cannot be formed or perfected.

LESSON 6 STUDY QUESTIONS BASED ON "THE SPIRIT-FILLED LIFE — FRUIT AND MANIFESTATIONS"

1. What is "The Spirit-Filled Life"?
2. How does the Spirit-filled life find expression?
3. What is meant by "The Fruit of the Spirit"?
4. Why does it say fruit, rather than fruits?
5. How can we produce the fruit of the Spirit?
6. What is the nine-fold fruit of the Spirit that Christ desires to produce in and through us?
7. What are the gifts or manifestations of the Spirit?
8. How may we receive spiritual gifts?
9. Can a person merit a spiritual manifestation or gift?
10. Why must each member know his place in the Body of Christ?
11. Is it necessary to have the gifts of the Spirit operative in the church?

LESSON 7: THE SPIRIT-FILLED LIFE – PRAYER AND WORSHIP

1. **WHAT IS PRAYER?**

   Prayer is talking to God. As a person expresses his feelings in conversation with God, the prayer may take on the form of adoration, confession, supplication or thanksgiving. 1 Timothy 2:1, 8.

2. **HOW CAN A PERSON LEARN TO PRAY?**

   Every Christian should learn to pray; however, prayer cannot be "taught" like an academic subject. "Like love and faith, like the response of the soul to beauty and the experience of the joy of God, prayer has to be known at first hand or it is not known at all." (White)

   A. Prayer is learned through fellowship with those who pray and through reflection upon their example. It was "as Jesus was praying in a certain place, when He ceased" that one of the disciples was stirred to ask Him, "Lord, teach us to pray" (Luke 11:1). We learn to pray by listening to those of our spiritual friends who do pray; also, we learn by studying the Bible's account of the men of prayer to whom God was real and near and attentive.

   B. Prayer is learned through personal trial and error. Just as a growing child learns to please or displease his parents, so the developing Christian learns to harmonize his will with that of God. The beginning Christian should simply talk to God as he would with a friend, expressing his feelings right from his heart. James 4:3.

3. **IS THERE ANY BENEFIT IN MEMORIZED PRAYER?**

   Generally, a memorized prayer comes from the mind rather than the heart. Real prayer must be fervent and filled with faith. James 5:16; Hebrews 11:6. There are times when a memorized prayer is genuine, but usually the spontaneous prayer of the heart is better. Even the "Lord's Prayer" is given more for a general pattern ("After this manner," Matthew 6:9) than for exact repetition.

4. **PRAYER CAN BE ALONE OR WITH OTHERS PRESENT.**

   A. Every Christian should learn to pray alone, closeted off from any outside disturbing influence. Matthew 6:6; James 5:13; Acts 9:40; 10:9.

   B. Every Christian should learn to pray with the Church. Note that the influence of the world is still shut out, but you are blending your faith with that of other Christians. Matthew 18:20; Acts 4:24, 31; 12:5, 12; 13:3; 14:23; 16:13, 16; 20:36; 21:5.

5. **HOW DOES THE BAPTISM WITH THE HOLY GHOST AFFECT OUR PRAYER LIFE!**

   Tremendously! When the Holy Spirit dwells within us, a whole new

146

dimension of prayer is opened to us. A Spirit-baptized believer will still pray in the ordinary way, but on occasion the Spirit of God will HIMSELF pray through the person. This is called "praying in the Holy Ghost." Jude 20; Ephesians 6:18; Romans 8:26, 27; 1 Corinthians 14:15.

6. HOW DO YOU KNOW WHEN YOU ARE PRAYING IN THE HOLY GHOST?
When you are praying in tongues, you are actually praying in the Spirit. 1 Corinthians 14:2, 14, 15. This is why a person is so edified (strengthened or built up), 1 Corinthians 14:4. This is one of the most important works of the Spirit in the believer's life. As you yield your tongue, your body and your total being, your prayer then becomes the very prayer of the Holy Spirit. IT WILL BE ANSWERED!

7. WHAT IS WORSHIP?
Worship is expressing love to God. Worship involves reverence, adoration, respect, honor, devotion — but all of these things find their greatest fulfillment in the love-making of the human soul to God.

8. HOW CAN A PERSON LEARN TO WORSHIP GOD?
The way in which we are to worship God is carefully outlined for us in the Bible. Whereas prayer is taught in the Bible through illustration of men's lives, worship is outlined in a very factual way.

9. WHY IS THE BIBLE SO SPECIFIC ABOUT THE WAY IN WHICH WE WORSHIP?
Most men have some desire to worship the Almighty. Invariably, however, when men are left to their own devices they worship God incorrectly. The great burden of the prophets was to keep the people from idolatry and corrupted worship. To insure proper worship and to safeguard our spiritual welfare, the Bible is definite in its teaching on HOW we should worship.

10. WHERE IN THE BIBLE DO YOU FIND TEACHING ON WORSHIP?
Worship, like prayer, runs throughout the Bible; however, the book of Psalms (the longest book of the Bible) was placed in the Bible for the specific purpose of teaching us how to worship.

11. SHOULD WE NEW TESTAMENT CHRISTIANS ACCEPT PSALMS AS AN AUTHORITY?
Yes. Jesus confirmed the boisterous praise of the children by quoting Psalms 8:2 (Matthew 21:16). Jesus and the apostles sang a psalm together before His death and then also after His resurrection Jesus continues to sing and fulfill the psalms by singing through the praises of the Church (Mark 14:26; Hebrews 2:12; Psalms 22:22). Paul linked his Christ-centered way of worshipping with the teaching of the Law and the Prophets (Acts 24:14). Paul writes to the Roman Gentile Church and in telling them how they can glorify God, he refers twice to David and once to Moses (Romans 15:9-11;

Psalms 18:49; 117:1; Deuteronomy 32:43). Paul twice exhorts the New Testament Churches to use the psalmic method of praise (Colossians 3:17; Ephesians 5:19). Finally, the Book of Revelation — which shows us the perfected will of God in Heaven — thunders with the same praise and adoration that is taught in the book of Psalms; John, the writer of Revelation, is admonished to "worship God" (Revelation 19:10), and obviously he should worship in the same way that he sees those in the heavenlies worshipping.

12. HOW SHOULD WE WORSHIP GOD?

With the mind directed to the Lord in adoration, the mouth, the hands and the body can find nine-fold expression:

	1. Singing — Psalms 9:2, 11; 13:6; 40:3.	
MOUTH	2. Audible Praise — Psalms 103:1; 117:1, 2.	
	3. Shouting — Psalms 47:1.	
	4. Lifting — Psalms 28:2; 63:4; 119:48; 134:2; 141:2.	
HANDS	5. Clapping — Psalms 47:1.	
	6. Musical Instruments — Psalms 150.	
	7. Standing — Psalms 134:1; 135:2.	
BODY	8. Bowing, Prostrating — Psalms 95:6.	
	9. Dancing — Psalms 30:11; 149:3; 150:4.	

13. HOW DOES THE BAPTISM WITH THE HOLY GHOST AFFECT OUR WORSHIP?

Tremenedously! Jesus teaches that His Spirit will bring new life to worship (John 4:23; 6:63). Paul clearly defines the New Testament Church as one that worships "in the spirit" (Philippians 3:3); he also links Ephesians 5:19 (which discusses worship) with "be filled with the Spirit" (v. 18). The term "spiritual songs" suggests songs born spontaneously of the Spirit (Colossians 3:16; Ephesians 5:19). We can sing with the Spirit (1 Corinthians 14:15). Allowing the Holy Spirit to quicken within us the Davidic forms of worship is truly a thrilling and inspiring experience.

LESSON 7 STUDY QUESTIONS BASED ON
"THE SPIRIT-FILLED LIFE — PRAYER AND WORSHIP"

1. What is prayer?
2. How can a person learn to pray?
3. Is there any benefit in memorized prayer?
4. Can prayer be alone or with others present?
5. How does the Baptism with the Holy Ghost affect'our prayer life?

6. How do you know when you are praying in the Holy Ghost?
7. What is worship?
8. How can a person learn to worship God?
9. Why is the Bible so specific about the way in which we worship?
10. Where in the Bible do you find teaching on worship?
11. Should we New Testament Christians accept Psalms as an authority?
12. How should we worship God?
13. How does the Baptism with the Holy Ghost affect our worship?

LESSON 8: CONFIRMATION AND THE LAYING ON OF HANDS

1. **WHAT IS CONFIRMATION?**

   The dictionary defines "confirmation" as an act of being made firm or firmer; being established or strengthened.

   The religious definition, which we will use, is as follows: "Confirmation is a solemn rite of the church whereby members are settled, strengthened and established in the faith as it is in Christ Jesus."

Acts 14:21, 22	— "Confirming the souls of the disciples."
Acts 15:41	— "Judas and Silas . . . exhorted . . . and confirmed them."
1 Corinthians 1:5, 6	— "Even as the testimony of Christ was confirmed."

2. **HOW IS THE RITE OF CONFIRMATION ADMINISTERED?**

   The rite of confirmation is administered through the laying on of the hands of the presbytery; the presbytery is composed of the governing body of ministers (elders) of the Church.

Acts 6:6	— "When they had prayed, they laid their hands on them."
Acts 13:3	— "When they had fasted and prayed, and laid their hands . . ."
1 Timothy 4:14	— "The gift . . . with the laying on of the hands of the presbytery."

3. **WHO MAY BE CONFIRMED?**

   Spirit-filled believers may be confirmed after they have been instructed in the doctrine and ordinances of the Bible so that they may be worthy members of the Church of Jesus Christ.

4. **IS THERE MORE THAN ONE CONFIRMATION FOR BELIEVERS?**

   Yes, there are steps in confirmation which may be experienced one at a time. These steps fall into three classes:

   A. **SIMPLE CONFIRMATION.** After a new convert has had a period of instruction in the basic truths of Christ and the Bible, there should be a public acknowledgment that he now understands what is expected of him as a disciple. At the conclusion of this catechism course, we will publicly lay hands on those who have demonstrated their grasp of the doctrines taught. This experience will help establish the believer in the faith of the Lord Jesus Christ — both publicly and personally. 1 Corinthians 1:5, 6; 2 Timothy 3:14.

   B. **CONFIRMATION WITH PROPHECY.** This experience should be for those who are ready to begin a spiritual function and ministry for the Lord. A presbytery of proven ministers (preferably visiting ministers) from outside the local church) should lay hands on each candidate and through Divine wisdom and prophetic utterance give each believer a confirmation of their spiritual calling and an impartation of spiritual gifts. 1 Timothy 1:18; 4:14; 2 Timothy 1:6; Acts 13:1-4. Old Testament: Genesis 48:14; Deuteronomy 34:9.

NOTE: This experience should occur after fasting and prayer, and the person upon whom hands are laid should be a dedicated Christian in the local church. And, not just anyone should be allowed to minister to others in confirmation. 1 Timothy 5:22. This experience is to be before the local church, not in an isolated, unauthorized meeting.

C.   CONFIRMATION AT ORDINATION. When a person is ready to enter the full-time ministry, the presbytery should lay hands on him and ordain him. Acts 6:6; 13:1-4.

5.   SHOULD ALL BELIEVERS SEEK CONFIRMATION?
Yes. Confirmation is one of the means the Spirit employs to make the will of God known to us. Romans 1:11; 12:2.

6.   WHAT ARE THE BLESSINGS OF CONFIRMATION?
The blessings of confirmation are these:

A.   It strengthens and establishes us in the faith.

B.   It binds us to the will and purpose of God.

C.   It causes the believer to assume responsibility in the local church, and it causes the congregation to acknowledge the spiritual life and ministry of the individual.

D.   Many times the Holy Spirit will speak through the presbytery and commission the recipient to a particular ministry in the Church of Jesus Christ.

E.   Spiritual gifts and graces are imparted to the recipient by the laying on of the hands of the presbytery when a commission accompanies the rite of confirmation.

7.   ARE THE GIFTS AND CALLINGS OF GOD FOR EVERYONE?
Every Spirit-filled believer has a place to fulfill in God's program, but it should be noted that the gifts and callings of God are according to His purpose; we should also note that we must sanctify ourselves unto the purposes of God. Everyone is urged to sanctify himself unto the Lord but everyone does not do so. The Holy Spirit who searches the hearts, separates unto His service by confirmation those whose hearts He sees are amply prepared. 1 Corinthians 2:10, 11; 12; Psalms 139:23, 24.

151

8. **WHAT IS THE REASON THAT THE GIFTS AND CALLINGS OF GOD DO NOT ALWAYS ACCOMPANY CONFIRMATION?**

   The gifts and callings of God that come through prophecy at confirmation are dependent upon the recipient's attitude and sanctification. Romans 12:2.

9. **HOW CAN STRENGTH, ESTABLISHMENT, SPIRITUAL GIFTS AND GRACES BE IMPARTED BY THE LAYING ON OF HANDS AND PROPHECY?**

   Through the laying on of hands and prophecy, there is an impartation of the creative Spirit of God which strengthens and establishes His people. By the inspired word of prophecy, spiritual gifts and graces are spoken into being. God will go to great lengths to fulfill the word of His prophets. 1 Timothy 1:18; 4:14; 1 Thessalonians 5:19-21; 2 Chronicles 20:20.

   Moses imparted wisdom to Joshua, Numbers 17:15-23; Deuteronomy 31:7, 8; 34:9.
   Elijah imparted a double portion to Elisha, 2 Kings 2:9-15.

10. **WHAT IS THE VOW WE RENEW WITH GOD IN CONFIRMATION?**

    The vow we renew with God in confirmation is the vow made by our parents in dedication — our life is dedicated for service to God and His Kingdom. Ecclesiastes 5:4, 5.

    "The God of all grace, who hath called us unto his eternal glory by Christ Jesus . . . make you perfect, stablish, strengthen, settle you. To Him be glory and dominion for ever and ever. Amen." 1 Peter 5:10, 11.

    "For God hath not given us the spirit of fear; but of power, and of love, and of a sound mind." 2 Timothy 1:7.

LESSON 8 STUDY QUESTIONS BASED ON "CONFIRMATION AND THE LAYING ON OF HANDS"

1. What is confirmation?
2. How is the rite of confirmation administered?
3. Who may be confirmed?
4. Is there more than one confirmation for believers?
5. Should all believers seek confirmation?
6. What are the blessings of confirmation?
7. Are the gifts and callings of God for everyone?
8. What is the reason that the gifts and callings of God do not always accompany confirmation?
9. How can strength, establishment, spiritual gifts and graces be imparted by the laying on of hands and prophecy.
10. What is the vow we renew with God in confirmation?

LESSON 9: RESURRECTION LIFE FOR MAN'S BODY

NOTE: This is the last lesson in Section VII, "The Life and Ministry of the Holy Spirit." In this Section, we have traced the work of the Holy Spirit in all of the Christian's basic experiences with God. We now study the climax! Just as Jesus was conceived of the Holy Spirit, was baptized with the Holy Spirit, etc., and was finally raised from the dead by the Spirit — so we too will reach the apex of the Spirit's work in our lives when we conquer death itself and are resurrected or translated!

1. **WHAT IS A RESURRECTION?**
   Resurrection is the raising of a dead body to life again. Obviously, this could only occur by Divine miracle.

2. **DOES THE BIBLE RECORD THAT ANYONE WAS EVER RAISED FROM THE DEAD?**
   Yes, the Bible records the following resurrections:

   In the Old Testament:
   > The Shunammite's son, 2 Kings 4:32-37.
   > A Moabite man, 2 Kings 13:20-21.
   > Moses, Deuteronomy 34:6; Luke 9:30; Jude 9.

   In the New Testament:
   > Jairus' Daughter, Matthew 9:18-26; Mark 5:22-43; Luke 8:41-56.
   > Widow's Son, at Nain, Luke 7:11-15.
   > Lazarus at Bethany, John 11:1-44.
   > Jesus Himself, Matthew 28:6; Mark 16:6; Luke 24:6; John 20.
   > Saints buried in Jerusalem, Matthew 27:51-53.
   > Peter raised Dorcas, Acts 9:36-42.

   NOTE: Although only the above mentioned resurrections are recorded in the Gospels, there probably were others. Matthew 10:8. Also, it should be noted that all of these individuals (except Moses and Jesus) lived as humans, and then died again.

3. **WHAT PURPOSE WAS SERVED BY THESE RESURRECTIONS?**
   Man's greatest and final enemy is death. 1 Corinthians 15:26. The above recorded miracles show forth God's present power and ultimate intention. It gives us a foretaste of the change to be experienced by the entire Church at Jesus' Second Coming.

4. **WHAT DO THE SCRIPTURES TEACH OF THE RESURRECTION OF THE BODY?**
   The Bible teaches that every human being that has died will be raised to life again, regardless of where and how the body was buried. John 5:28, 29; Revelation 20:12, 13.

153

5. WILL THERE BE ANY DIFFERENCE BETWEEN OUR FUTURE RESUR-
RECTION AND THE RESURRECTIONS THAT ARE RECORDED UNDER
QUESTION 2?
Yes, there will be a significant difference. For instance, when Jesus raised
Lazarus from the dead, a miracle of creation took place. Putrefaction had
already begun in the corpse. The command of Jesus produced the mirac-
ulous reconstruction of the body cells. Lazarus, however, was only given
another functional human body — which eventually died agian.

Jesus, on the other hand, came forth from the tomb with a different type
of resurrection body. Rather than blood flowing through His body to sustain
His life, the very Spirit of God moved through every cell and organ imparting
the fullness of eternal life. This is why Jesus could appear and disappear and
pass through solid walls in His resurrected body. Luke 24:31; John 20:19.
This is the type of body that we will have in the resurrection; rather than a
body that could die again and that would require physical food and care,
we will be nourished and sustained by the very power of eternal life that
brought Jesus forth out of the grave. Romans 8:11; 1 Corinthians 15:50-54.

6. HOW MANY RESURRECTIONS WILL THERE BE?
There will be two resurrections, commonly known as the First and Second
Resurrections. Revelation 20:6.
"All that are in the graves shall hear His voice, and shall come forth;
they that have done good, unto the resurrection of life; and they that
have done evil, unto the resurrection of damnation." John 5:28, 29.

7. WHEN WILL THE FIRST RESURRECTION OCCUR?
The First Resurrection will happen at the Second Coming of the Lord Jesus
Christ. This glorious appearing of Jesus will be at the conclusion of the 6th
Day of God's "Plan of the Ages" (see Section III on Dispensational Truth)
and will bring in the 1,000 years of Peace (commonly known as "The
Millennium"). 1 Thessalonians 4:33-17.

8. WILL ANYONE BE ALIVE WHEN JESUS COMES AGAIN?

A. Some of God's children will be alive, for Paul states that "we which
ARE ALIVE and REMAIN unto the coming of the Lord . . . shall be
caught up together with them in the cloud." 1 Thessalonians 4:15-18.

B. The same glory that draws the living and dead in Christ at His Second
Coming shall also destroy the wicked. 2 Thessalonians 1:7-10.

9. WHEN WILL THE SECOND RESURRECTION OCCUR?

A. There is a great diversity of opinion on the teaching of the First and
Second Resurrections. Not only do Bible teachers disagree about who

154

is in the Resurrections, but also there is great disagreement about the time when these Resurrections will take place.

B. This author feels that the Second Resurrection is at the end of the Millennium and that it is the raising of the ungodly dead. One thousand years separate the raising of the Godly and the ungodly. Revelation 20. The wicked dead will be judged at their resurrection and put into the Lake of Fire. Revelation 20:14, 15.

10. WHERE ARE THE DEAD NOW?
The bodies of all the dead are in the grave. The souls of the righteous are in heaven with Jesus Christ. 2 Corinthians 5:8; Philippians 1:23. The souls of the ungodly are in Sheol or Hades (translated as "hell"). Revelation 20:13.

11. WILL THE WICKED SOULS IN HADES BE GIVEN A CHANCE TO REPENT?
No. In Hades (or "hell") they await final judgment because they refused to accept God's offer of salvation and eternal life. There is no opportunity given for salvation after death. Hebrews 9:27; 2 Peter 2:9; John 3:16, 18; Luke 16:19-31. We should not and cannot pray for the wicked dead, since it would be meaningless prayer.

12. WHOM WILL GOD JUDGE AT THE LAST DAY?
Every man that ever lived will be judged at the last day. Revelation 20:12, 13; Matthew 25:31, 32; 2 Corinthians 5:10.

LESSON 9 STUDY QUESTIONS BASED ON "RESURRECTION LIFE FOR MAN'S BODY"

1. What is resurrection?
2. Does the Bible record that anyone was ever raised from the dead?
3. What purpose was served by these resurrections?
4. What do the scriptures teach of the resurrection of the body?
5. Will there be any difference between our future resurrection and the resurrections that are recorded under question 2?
6. How many resurrections will there be?
7. When will the First Resurrection occur?
8. Will anyone be alive when Jesus comes again?
9. When will the Second Resurrection occur?
10. Where are the dead now?
11. Will the wicked souls in Hades be given a chance to repent?
12. Whom will God judge at the last day?

PART VIII.
THE MINISTRY AND WORK OF THE CHURCH

PART VIII. THE MINISTRY AND WORK OF THE CHURCH

PART VIII. THE MINISTRY AND WORK OF THE CHURCH

LESSON 1: THE CHURCH – BOTH UNIVERSAL AND LOCAL

1. **WHAT WAS THE MEANING OF THE WORD "CHURCH" IN BIBLE DAYS?**
    The Greek word "ekklesia" which is translated "church" in our Bibles was not originally a religious term. It referred to the registered voters or citizens of a Greek city; these "called out" ones were the recognized voice of the city's political life. Both Jesus and Paul coined this word for its ready application to men and women who were "called out" of the world to become members of the Kingdom of God. Every truly dedicated follower of the Lord Jesus Christ was thereby considered a part of Christ's Church. Matthew 16:18.

2. **WHY ARE THERE SO MANY CHRISTIAN CHURCHES TODAY? WHICH IS RIGHT?**
    The true church must be exactly what the Bible declares it to be – as it was interpreted by Jesus and the early apostles. Unfortunately, during the past Church Age there have been many groups whose emphasis has shifted from the literal, dynamic interpretation of the Bible; they became side-tracked on some "special-interest" doctrinal interpretation. Often, too, church groups "cool off" in their fervency for God, and they change to become more acceptable in their community's life. We must say, therefore, that the great number of different churches represent the various divergent "off-center" interpretations of the Bible as well as various levels of spirituality. 2 Timothy 4:3, 4; Hebrews 2:1; 2 Peter 3:3; Jude 18.

    WHICH IS RIGHT? This must be your decision. May we suggest a simple approach in determining this? Imagine yourself back in Bible days as you read God's Word. Don't allow your own interpretations to creep in, or don't be influenced by the multitude of modern churches. Take the total Bible – with its own built in commentary – as your sole guide of what the Church should be. Then, associate with those Christians who come closest to that standard! 1 Thessalonians 2:13; Jude 3; 1 Timothy 4:16. Remember the principle of Matthew 9:16, 17.

3. **WHAT IS THE UNIVERSAL CHURCH?**
    Throughout the world every genuine believer in the Lord Jesus Christ that is walking in New Covenant relationship is part of the world-wide fellowship of His Church. This great Church is not denominational or political, but rather is united in Spiritual oneness. Ephesians 4:3-6; John 10:16. This many-membered Church is the Body of Christ.

4. **WHAT IS THE LOCAL CHURCH?**
    Every population area deserves at least one church that is actively participating in genuine Bible Christianity. The vision of the world-wide Church

is essential, but without a workable, tangible expression in every-day living. Christianity becomes meaningless. The local Church, then, becomes the focal point for the Christians of a given area as they minister to God, one another and the world. 1 Corinthians 11:18, 20; 14:23, 26. Note Revelation 2 and 3, the letters to the churches.

5. WHY DOES THE LOCAL CHURCH NEED A MEETING PLACE?
It is necessary for people to gather in a recognized place if they are to:

A. Assume responsibility in ministering to their community.

B. Maintain spiritual unity among themselves in promoting God's program in their local area.

C. Recognize leadership ministries that God has given and submit to apostolic authority.

D. Experience the wonders of congregational worship, prayer and communion.

E. Influence their children in the habits, disciplines and sacraments of Christian living and cooperation.

NOTE: Acts 2:1, 42, 46; 4:23, 31; 12:5, 12; 13:1; 15:20, 36,41; 18:7; 19:9; 20:7, 20.

6. THE CLOSET CONCEPT APPLIED TO THE CHURCH'S MEETING PLACE.
Jesus taught the importance of personal, secluded "closet" praying, Matthew 6:6. Church meetings should also be "closet" experiences — on the congregational level. When the church meets, the influence of the world should be shut out. It should be a gathering of the Body of Christ to glorify God, not just an effort to please the non-Christians. Hebrews 2:12.

7. WHY MEET TOGETHER AS A CHURCH?
When Christians leave their homes and jobs and journey to a central meeting place, they have a right to expect something greater than they could experience at home (or another church). For instance, every Christian should have wonderful times of prayer in his home — but it should be much greater to pray in the church's power-packed prayer meetings; Bible study at home should be climaxed by anointed teaching in the Church that is on a higher level than the individual could attain alone; congregational prayer and worship should be so thrilling and wonderful that no home experience could equal it! This "step-up" concept in spiritual experience is the best reason for people to become an active part of a local church.

LESSON 1 STUDY QUESTIONS BASED ON
"THE CHURCH — BOTH UNIVERSAL AND LOCAL"

1. What was the meaning of the word "church" in Bible days?
2. Why are there so many Christian Churches today? Which is right?
3. What is the universal Church?
4. What is the local church?
5. Why does the local church need a meeting place?
6. How is the "closet concept" applied to the church's meeting place?
7. Why meet together as a church?

LESSON 2: LEADERSHIP MINISTRIES IN THE CHURCH

1. THE FIVE LEADERSHIP MINISTRIES THAT CHRIST GAVE THE CHURCH ARE:

    Apostles, prophets, evangelists, pastors and teachers. Ephesians 4:8, 11, 12.

2. WHY ARE THESE FIVE MINISTRIES KNOWN AS THE "ASCENSION GIFT MINISTRIES"?

    As the text in Ephesians 4 indicates, these ministries are the gifts of the Lord Jesus Christ to His Church. The Lord Jesus could bestow these "gifts" as a direct result of His ascending from the earth to Heaven again.

3. CHRIST HAD A SPECIFIC PURPOSE IN GIVING THESE MINISTRIES TO THE CHURCH.

    Christ gave these basic, ascension gift ministries to the Church for her perfection, edification and strengthening.

    "for the perfecting of the saints, unto the work of ministering, unto the building up of the Body of Christ." Ephesians 4:12, R.V.

4. WE SHOULD EXPECT TO SEE THESE MINISTRIES IN THE CHURCH TODAY!

    These are days of spiritual restoration. Without these vital ministries the Church can never come into complete perfection. These ministries are a part of Christ's program and covenant; therefore, we can expect all of these ministries to function in the Church of the last days. The Church is now in the upward swing of restoration out of the tradition of the Dark Ages. She is being restored to the original apostolic power and glory as in the beginning.   Joel 1:4; 2:25;

5. THE MINISTRY OF THE APOSTLE.

    A. The word "apostle" means "one who is sent with a special commission." An apostle is an ambassador of Christ whose primary mission for the Kingdom of God is to establish congregations, both in the founding of new churches and also the strengthening of those already in existence. As an apostle founds a local church, he takes the oversight until the Holy Spirit prepares and reveals God's choice of a pastor and elders for them. In established churches the apostle ministers and presides in a church at the invitation of the pastor. In an advisory capacity, as well as in spiritual ministry, his ministry greatly strengthens the congregation.

    Acts 14:4, 14; 2 Corinthians 8:23; Philippians 2:25; Revelation 2:2.

    B. This is a ministry to the whole Body of Christ rather than to just one church. It is primarily a ministry of government, similar to that of a pastor except that it is on a greater scale. For instance, Paul was an apostle to the Gentiles (Galatians 1:1), and Peter was an apostle to the Jews (Galatians 2:7). This ministry utilizes the "word of wisdom" in particular. 1 Corinthians 12:8.

C. The seal of a man's apostleship is the fruit he has brought to the Lord. 1 Corinthians 9:2. "What has he been able to establish?" is the question to be asked in evaluating an apostle. The signs of the apostle will be patience, signs, wonders and a spiritual parental concern. An apostle will be a father of churches, a pastor of pastors, one who makes the final decisions on doctrine; one who is destined to suffer for His Name's sake.

Acts 2:42; 9:15, 16; 15:13, 22; 1 Corinthians 4:9-15; 2 Corinthians 12:12.

6. THERE WERE MORE THAN TWELVE APOSTLES IN THE NEW TESTAMENT. In addition to the original twelve apostles, we find the following seven men are also called by that title:

Matthias (Acts 1:26), Paul and Barnabas (Acts 14:1, 4, 14), Titus (2 Corinthians 8:23, Greek), Epaphroditus (Philippians 2:25), Silas and Timothy (1 Thessalonians 1:1; 2:6). In addition, it is possible that Andronicus and Junia were apostles (Romans 16:7).

7. THE MINISTRY OF THE PROPHET.

A. Sometimes the term "seer" is used in the Old Testament to describe this ministry. 1 Samuel 9:9-19; 2 Samuel 24:11; 1 Chronicles 9:22; 2 Chronicles 9:29; 12:15; 16:7; 19:2.

B. A prophet is one who speaks for God, bringing revelation and direction from God to the Church. The gift of prophecy and the word of knowledge will operate in the prophet; this will allow him to foretell the future or reveal present facts otherwise not known and to reveal the mind of God.

Acts 11:27, 28; 13:1; 15:32; 21:10, 11; 1 Corinthians 12:28.

C. The prophet has the ability to make the hidden truths and mysteries of God plain; he is a revealer of Truth. This is a ministry of revelation to the whole Body of Christ. Amos 3:7; Ephesians 3:3, 5. This ministry is the only one suitable for "directive prophecy."

D. The prophet will also prophesy in the Church in the more simple realm open to all believers; that is, the area of edification, exhortation and comfort. 1 Corinthians 14:3.

8. THE MINISTRY OF THE EVANGELIST.

An evangelist is a proclaimer of the good news of salvation. The gift of faith characterizes this ministry. Not only does the evangelist strengthen the Church and stir the believers, but also he is gifted with a strong public ministry in reaching the unsaved — an extension arm of the Church. Conviction will be with this ministry. Philip is a New Testament example.

Acts 8:5-8; 21:8; Ephesians 4:11; 2 Timothy 4:5.

9. THE MINISTRY OF THE PASTOR.

A. The pastor is the shepherd of the local church flock; a ministry of tender concern that cares for the spiritual state of the congregation — shepherding, correcting, admonishing, teaching and disciplining.

B. Each church should develop a multiple-ministry of elders (or bishops) who help in the oversight of the local spiritual program. The pastor is considered one of these elders, but the nature of his ministry makes him the overall director and supervisor of the activities and operations in the church.

C. The pastor is worthy of support that will enable him to be in the full-time ministry.

1 Timothy 5:17, 18; 1 Corinthians 9:9-14; Matthew 10:10; Luke 8:3.

D. This is not a traveling ministry, in the sense that the pastor is away for long periods of time. You never see a shepherd wandering all over the country, he stays with the sheep to care for them.

Jeremiah 3:15; Acts 20:28; Hebrews 13:17; 1 Peter 5:2, 3.

E. While an apostle is founding a local church or churches, he may reside in the area for a time and literally fulfil the ministry of a local pastor as well as that of an apostle. As, Paul in Ephesus for two years (Acts 19:10) or in Corinth for one and one-half years (Acts 18:11).

10. THE MINISTRY OF THE TEACHER

A. The ministry of a teacher is to explain, in easily understood terms, the things concerning God and His Word. The doctrine that comes to the Church through the wisdom and revelation of the apostles and prophets must be explained to the people in meaningful terms.

B. The teacher must guide the studies of the Church in sound, practical doctrine; he must train the Church for Christian action. The people must be challenged to DO the Word as well as hear it. The teacher must himself be a real student of the Bible with the anointed ability to receive revelation from the Word and impart it to others.

Nehemiah 8:7-12; Isaiah 28:9; Matthew 5:1, 2; Luke 24:27; John 7:14; Acts 13:1; Romans 12:7; 1 Corinthians 12:28; 1 Timothy 2:7.

C. The gift of teaching varies. The gift of one may be to teach the Word to children; another will be effective in teaching young people. A teacher may be only in the local church or a traveling ministry recognized by the whole Church.

11. WHAT IS THE MINISTRY OF AN ELDER?

An elder is a man of mature age and experience who is recognized as a spiritual overseer in the local church. Three terms are used to describe this ministry: "elder" describes the position and maturity; "bishop" describes the same ministry in terms of its function of oversight; "presbyter" comes from the same word as "elder" and means the same thing. The elders work in close harmony with the pastor in the shepherding of the local congregation. An elder should be a person whose ministry is one of the five "ascension gift ministries."

1 Timothy 3:1; 5:1, 17; Titus 1:5, 7; Acts 20:17; 28-30.

12. WHAT IS A PRESBYTERY?

The governing body of elders (ministers) in a local church is called a presbytery. Since one elder is a presbyter, a presbytery would refer to two or more presbyters or elders working together. 1 Timothy 4:14. When a visiting team of ministers come to visit a local church for prophetic ministry, they too constitute a presbytery; they would, of course, work in conjunction with the presbytery already established in that church.

13. THE MINISTRY OF THE DEACON AND DEACONESS.

The basic meaning of the original word is "servant" or "one who serves or waits on others." This is actually an advanced ministry of helps (1 Corinthians 12:28) designed to help the pastor and elders better perform their ministries. Attending to the poor, taking charge of the temporal needs of the local church, etc., are very vital tasks that must be done by responsible people.

1 Timothy 3:8; Acts 6:1-7; Romans 16:1, 2.

14. DOES A WOMAN HAVE A MINISTRY IN THE CHURCH?

In the Church, there is neither male nor female. Christ, who is the Head, anoints whom He will to operate the ministries in His Church.

Galatians 3:28; 1 Peter 4:10, 11.

15. DID NOT PAUL FORBID WOMEN TO SPEAK IN THE CHURCH?

In keeping with the customs of that day, the women were not to be talkative or unruly in the services. That the women did prophesy or teach is evident from Paul's words in 1 Corinthians 11:5 where he lays down rules to regulate the women's conduct while ministering in the Church. Joel 2:28, 29. Paul does forbid a woman to usurp authority over a man, but this refers to a woman being in subjection to her husband.

1 Timothy 2:11-13; Acts 21:8, 9; 9:36-42; 18:26.

LESSON 2 STUDY QUESTIONS BASED ON
"LEADERSHIP MINISTRIES IN THE CHURCH"

1. What are the leadership ministries Christ gave to the Church?
2. Why are these five ministries known as the "Ascension Gift Ministries"?
3. For what purpose did Christ give these ministries to the Church?
4. Should we expect to see these ministries in the Church today?
5. What is the ministry of an apostle?
6. Were there just 12 apostles in the New Testament?
7. What is the ministry of a prophet?
8. What is the ministry of an evangelist?
9. What is the ministry of a pastor?
10. What is the ministry of a teacher?
11. What is the ministry of an elder?
12. What is a presbytery?
13. What is the ministry of a deacon and deaconess?
14. Does a woman have a ministry in the Church?
15. Did not Paul forbid women to speak in the Church?

LESSON 3: DISCIPLINE IN THE CHURCH

1. **WHAT IS CHURCH DISCIPLINE?**
   Church Discipline is the corrective action that a church body must take to insure the proper conduct or behavior of its members.

2. **WHY IS IT NEEDED IN A CHURCH CONGREGATION?**
   Without discipline it is impossible to maintain properly the Church's fellowship with Christ and with one another. Communion is broken where sin exists. Romans 6:12, 13. Note Joshua 7:1 where the sin of one man affected all Israel.

3. **DOES GOD GIVE THE CHURCH POWER TO EXECUTE JUDGMENT? ISN'T GOD ALONE TO JUDGE HIS PEOPLE?**
   Although God Himself is the Judge of all mankind, He does delegate certain types of judgment to His Church.

   "the saints shall judge the world . . . are ye unworthy to judge the smallest matters? Know ye not that we shall judge angels? How much more things that pertain to this life?" 1 Corinthians 6:2, 3.

   "tell it to the Church" — Matthew 18:17.

4. **WHAT PLACE SHOULD PRAYER HAVE IN ALL MATTERS OF DISCIPLINE?**
   Prayer should come first, always. If the church is to act for Christ, she must know the mind and will of Christ. Prayer is the church's method of contacting Christ and determining His will. Matthew 18:18, 19.

5. **WHAT COURSE OF DISCIPLINE SHOULD BE TAKEN IF A BROTHER TRESPASS AGAINST ANOTHER?**
   When a difference exists between two brethren, the one who has been wronged is required to go to the one at fault and try to make reconciliation. Matthew 18:15.

6. **HOW MANY ATTEMPTS SHOULD BE MADE TO BRING RECONCILIATION?**
   Two attempts should be made privately, with witnesses present at the second attempt. Matthew 18:16.

7. **IF TWO ATTEMPTS FAIL, WHAT PROCEDURE SHOULD BE TAKEN?**

   After the failure of two attempts, the matter must be brought before the Church which is represented by the local congregation. Matthew 18:17.

8. **IF THE SINNING MEMBER WILL NOT HEED THE CHURCH'S ADVICE, WHAT IS THE NEXT PROCEDURE?**

   ". . . but if he neglect to hear the church, let him be unto thee as an heathen man and a publican." Matthew 18:17.

9. WHAT IS THE MAXIMUM DISCIPLINE WHICH THE CHURCH CAN IMPOSE?
   There are only two forms of discipline which the Church can impose:

   A.   The exclusion of a sinning member from the Lord's Supper.

   B.   The exclusion from the fellowship of believers. 1 Corinthians 5:11.

   NOTE: This is NOT an exclusion from the Body of Christ.

10. WHO DIRECTS THE PROCEDURE WHEN A CASE IS BROUGHT BEFORE THE CHURCH FOR DISCIPLINE?
    The elders are to take the initiative. Titus 1:9.

11. WHERE THERE ARE NO ELDERS, WHO TAKES THE INITIATIVE?
    Where there are no elders, those who are spiritual should take the initiative to see that correction is exercised. Galatians 6:1.

    NOTE: In every case, it is the local church that must assume the responsibility.

12. IF A MEMBER SINS OR TEACHES FALSE DOCTRINE, HOW SHOULD THE CHURCH DEAL WITH HIM ASSUMING THAT THE STEPS MENTIONED IN QUESTIONS 5 THROUGH 8 HAVE BEEN TAKEN?

    A.   A member who falls into sin should be taken from among the church. 1 Corinthians 5:3-5; 2 Thessalonians 3:6.

    B.   A member who teaches false doctrine should be rejected by the congregation. Titus 3:10; Romans 16:17; 2 John 10, 11.

13. WHEN THE CHARGE OF HERESY (FALSE TEACHING) IS BROUGHT AGAINST A CHURCH MEMBER, TWO THINGS SHOULD BE CONSIDERED:

    A.   Consider if the one concerned is wrong due to the fact that he is not fully instructed or misapprehends the meaning of the Scripture. Note: Acts 18:26.

    B.   Consider if it is doctrine that is heretical, Satanic in origin and accompanied by practices and doctrine that separates from fellowship with the Lord. 1 Timothy 6:3-5; 1:20; 2 Timothy 2:17, 18.

14. WHY IS A SINNING MEMBER DELIVERED TO SATAN?
    A sinning member is delivered unto Satan that he might be brought to repentance, that he might be saved — that he might learn not to blaspheme. 1 Corinthians 5:5b; 1 Timothy 1:20b.

15. SHOULD A CHURCH MEMBER, WHO HAS BEEN RESTORED, MAKE A PUBLIC CONFESSION OF SIN?
    The Scripture does not substantiate this. Detailed public confession of sin

is morally and spiritually hurtful to all, especially when just a few people are involved. If it is something of major consequence that involves the entire congregation's attention, a simple public statement by the elders will usually be sufficient.

16. **DOES THE CHURCH HAVE ANY AUTHORITY TO CHASTISE OR PUNISH ITS MEMBERS?**

No. The church has no authority to chastise or punish its members. This is God's business; only God can do it righteously. True repentance (which comes from God) brings cleansing and where this cleansing has taken place the church can do nothing but acknowledge it.

17. **WHAT ACTION IS TAKEN IN THE CASE OF A SINNING ELDER?**

An accusation against an Elder must not be received except before two or three witnesses. Then, if he is rebuked before the church, others are encouraged NOT to commit the same error. 1 Timothy 5:19, 20.

18. **WHAT STAND MUST THE CHURCH TAKE CONCERNING THE BELIEVER AND THE WORLD?**

The believer should not marry an unbeliever, nor enter into business partnerships with unbelievers that endanger his testimony. 2 Corinthians 6:14, 15; 1 Corinthians 7:39.

LESSON 3 STUDY QUESTIONS BASED ON "DISCIPLINE IN THE CHURCH"

1. What is Church discipline?
2. Why is it needed in a church congregation?
3. Does God give the Church power to execute judgment? Isn't God alone to judge His people?
4. What place should prayer have in all matters of discipline?
5. What course of discipline should be taken if a brother trespass against another?
6. How many attempts should be made to bring reconciliation?
7. If two attempts fail, what procedure should be taken?
8. If the sinning member will not heed the church's advice, what is the next procedure?
9. What is the maximum discipline which the church can impose?
10. Who directs the procedure when a case is brought before the church for discipline?
11. Where there are no elders, who takes the initiative?
12. If a member sins or teaches false doctrine, how should the church deal with him assuming that the steps mentioned in questions 5 through 8 have been taken?
13. When the charge of heresy (false teaching) is brought against a church member, what two things should be considered?

14. Why is a sinning member delivered to Satan?
15. Should a church member, who has been restored, make a public confession of sin?
16. Does the church have any authority to chastise or punish its members?
17. What action is taken in the case of a sinning elder?
18. What stand must the church take concerning the believer and the world?

LESSON 4: THE SACRAMENT OF COMMUNION IN THE CHURCH

1. WHAT IS THE MEANING OF THE WORD "COMMUNION"?
    The dictionary definition of this word suggests: "Act of sharing; communication; mutual intercourse; unity, concord, agreement; participation."

2. WHAT IS THE SACRAMENT OF COMMUNION PRACTICED BY THE CHURCH?
    Although Christians enjoy communion with Christ through the Holy Spirit, there is a sacred act which each Christian can do WITH the Church which lifts "communion" to a higher level. The re-creation of "The Lord's Supper" in the New Testament Church through the use of bread and "the fruit of the vine" brings Christ's living presence in a very special way.

3. VARIOUS TITLES ARE GIVEN TO THIS SACRAMENT IN THE CHURCH.
    It is called "The Communion," "Holy Communion," "The Sacrament," "The Lord's Supper," "The Eucharist." The names and procedure vary in the different churches.

4. WHERE DID THE COMMUNION ORIGINATE?
    God gave Israel a series of feasts throughout their calendar year which commemorated great truths. The first feast of the year was called "The Passover" (Exodus 12), and brought a yearly reminder to God's people that it was through the blood and body of the lamb that Israel was delivered from Egyptian bondage. Jesus kept this feast with his disciples (in the Jewish tradition) on the night before His crucifixion. He then transformed the Passover of the Old Covenant into the Communion of the New Covenant — making His own body and blood the fulfillment of the Passover Lamb. Matthew 26:17-30; Mark 14:12-25; Luke 22:1-20; John 13.

5. WHAT IS THE DIFFERENCE BETWEEN THE PASSOVER AND THE COMMUNION SERVICE?
    The Passover was actually a meal in which a lamb was roasted and eaten and served with bitter herbs, unleavened bread and wine. Jesus eliminated the "dinner" aspect of the Passover, and simply requested his disciples to partake of the Bread and the Cup at future gatherings as a remembrance of His Body and Blood. Luke 22:19; 1 Corinthians 11:24, 25:

6. SHOULD THE COMMUNION SERVICE FOLLOW SOME SPECIAL FORM?
    The teaching of Jesus and Paul indicate that Communion should be kept as simple and spiritual as possible. It should be done with other Christians (1 Corinthians 11:20, 34); it should follow a time of heart searching and prayer (1 Corinthians 11:28), so that those participating really discern the meaning of the Lord's Body and Blood. Gathering together in spiritual oneness (1 Corinthians 11:33), the Christians first partake of the broken bread together and then partake of the Cup together. (1 Corinthians 11:26).

171

7. HOW OFTEN SHOULD THE CHURCH SERVE COMMUNION?

Paul said, "as often as ye eat this bread, and drink this cup, ye do shew . . ." (1 Corinthians 11:26) which indicates that Communion can be very frequent. It is possible that the early Church partook of Communion every week (Acts 2:42, 46; 20:7, 11; note that "breaking of bread" also refers to the ordinary meal). The Communion should be kept frequently, but we should not allow it to become a mechanical ritual.

8. WHAT HAPPENS TO A PERSON WHEN HE PARTAKES OF COMMUNION?

Jesus clearly teaches in John 6:52-63 that we must eat His flesh and drink His blood. Verses 62 and 63 show that it is not a material feeding on His Body and Blood, but rather a spiritual participation. Jesus and Paul gave no great explanation of any chemical changes, etc. Jesus simply said, "This is my body" and "This is my blood." As we seek the Lord in faith during Communion, God's Spirit imparts spiritual revelation and life in a way that defies interpretation.

9. CAN ANYONE PARTAKE WITH THE CHURCH OF THE COMMUNION?

No. The Communion is definitely NOT for sinners. Only those Christians who are in covenant relationship with God should partake. Every participating Christian should search his own heart to be sure that he does not have ought against anyone or is not in rebellion against Christ. 1 Corinthians 11:28.

10. WHAT ARE THE CONSEQUENCES OF PARTICIPATING IN COMMUNION?

For the unworthy:

"guilty of the body and blood of the Lord" — 1 Corinthians 11:27.
"eateth and drinketh damnation to himself" — 1 Corinthians 11:29.
"for this cause many are weak and sickly among you, and many sleep (are dead)" — 1 Corinthians 11:30.
"Ye have no life in you" — John 6:53.

For the worthy:

"Ye do shew (proclaim) the Lord's death till he come" — 1 Corinthians 11:26.
"hath eternal life" and "he shall live by me" — John 6:54, 57.
"in remembrance of me" — 1 Corinthians 11:24, 25.

LESSON 4 STUDY QUESTIONS BASED ON "THE SACRAMENT OF COMMUNION"

1. What is the meaning of the word "Communion"?
2. What is the Sacrament of Communion practiced by the Church?

LESSON 4 STUDY QUESTIONS BASED ON
"THE SACRAMENT OF COMMUNION" (Continued)

3. List several other titles for this Sacrament.
4. Where did the Communion originate?
5. What is the difference between the Passover and the Communion?
6. Should the Communion Service follow some special form?
7. How often should the church serve Communion?
8. What happens to a person when he partakes of Communion?
9. Can anyone partake with the church of the Communion?
10. What are the consequences of partaking of the Communion?

PART IX.
OUR PERSONAL CHRISTIAN RESPONSIBILITY

PART IX.   CHRISTIAN RESPONSIBILITY

PART IX. CHRISTIAN RESPONSIBILITY

LESSON 1: MARRIAGE IS A SACRAMENT

1. DEFINE THE MEANING OF "SACRAMENT."

   A "sacrament" is a holy action performed in and by the Church to fulfill Christ's command. No sacrament was meant to be a lifeless ceremony. Jesus kept the commanded sacraments of the Church to a bare minimum — knowing that the carnal man tends to glory in ritual more than in true consecration. When properly performed, the Bible sacraments are charged with spiritual reality and power.

2. WHAT IS THE SACRAMENT OF MARRIAGE?

   The Sacrament of Marriage is a covenant publicly made between a man, a woman and God for the purpose of founding and maintaining a family. God intends for such a covenant to be a lifelong union between husband and wife that can be dissolved only by death or unfaithfulness. Although couples legally may be united in marriage by civil authori-

   ties, Christians should consider their action a sacrament of the Church. Standing before God's minister and proper witnesses, the couple publicly make a sacred act of their mutual troth to one another.

   "What God hath joined together, let not man put asunder." Matthew 19:6.

   The above triangle signifies the three-fold covenant of marriage. It illustrates that a man's relationship should be as strong toward his God as toward his wife, and the wife's relationships should be equally strong. Children produced by such a marriage will be held steady within the sanctifying influence of the covenant boundaries.

3. WHAT PREPARATION DOES GOD REQUIRE OF THOSE ENTERING MARRIAGE?

   Since marriage is a Divine institution, the couple involved should properly begin with rightful betrothal or engagement. This should be done prayerfully, soberly and with purity of body and soul to insure compatibility.

   Institution of Marriage, Genesis 2:18-24; a wife for Isaac, Genesis 24:12. Although Joseph and Mary were only engaged, they were considered husband and wife. Matthew 1:19, 20, 24.

4. ENGAGED COUPLES SHOULD SEEK COMPATIBILITY OF SPIRIT AND EMOTION.

   Too many marriages are based on the Hollywood myth that physical satisfaction is paramount. Actually marriage involves more than sex. God also made men and women with spiritual, mental and emotional functions and needs. When a pre-marital relationship starts on the level of sexual fulfillment and attempts to move upward to spiritual fulfillment, it is pre-destined to trouble. However, if an engaged couple will concentrate first on establishing their spiritual and emotional compatibility, they can then come to a satisfying physical fulfillment in proper marriage.

5. WHEN ARE TWO PEOPLE CONSIDERED COMPATIBLE IN MARRIAGE?

Two people are compatible in marriage when they can live together in harmony and peace with God's blessing.

"God hath called us to peace." 1 Corinthians 7:15.

6. THERE ARE TWO BASIC MARRIAGE LAWS WHICH SHOULD NOT BE VIOLATED.

A. Christians are NOT permitted to marry unbelievers. 2 Corinthians 6:14; Deuteronomy 7:3, 4.

B. The Marriage Covenant is for a lifetime. Romans 7:2, 3.

7. HOW DOES GOD REGARD DIVORCE?

God is grieved when a marriage breaks up. In mercy the Lord permitted—with careful restrictions — the granting of a divorce in both Old Testament (Mark 10:4; Matthew 5:31; Deuteronomy 24:1) and also New Testament (Matthew 5:32; 1 Corinthians 7:15). Jesus taught, however, that God originally intended that a husband and wife should not be separated or "put asunder" (Mark 10:4-9).

8. WHAT ARE THE MAJOR REASONS FOR DIVORCE IN OUR SOCIETY?

Worldly people file for divorce with various reasons. Terms such as "mental cruelty," "incompatibility," "habitual drunkenness," etc., are frequently used. Actually these are mere excuses for deeper problems which can be traced to:

[1] Sexual incompatibility.

[2] Disagreement about earning and spending money; the problem of the working wife.

[3] Religious differences.

[4] Immaturity in making realistic decisions and handling the problems of life.

[5] Personal insecurity which is compounded by marriage to another insecure individual.

9. THE SAME REASONS MOTIVATE CHRISTIANS TO SEPARATE!

Christians should closely guard their marriages against the above mentioned problems. If the Spirit of Christ is maintained in both hearts, any of these marriage-breakers will lose its influence. Love always triumphs!

10. DOES GOD EVER GIVE PERMISSION TO DISSOLVE THE MARRIAGE COVENANT?

According to the Lord Jesus Christ, only one offense will justifiably warrant the annulment of the marriage covenant. Fornication — illicit sexual relations — is justifiable grounds for divorce. Matthew 19:9.

11. AT THIS POINT LET US CONSIDER TWO IMPORTANT DIFFERENCES BETWEEN THE SOCIETY OF BIBLE TIMES AND THE PRESENT.

A. In both Old Testament and New Testament times, polygamy was an accepted way of life; therefore, men did not always think in terms of divorcing one woman in order to get another — he simply added another wife. Even if a man were to lose his wife through divorce, he possibly would still have another wife living with him! Note Jacob in Genesis 29. Paul in the New Testament wisely instructs that bishops and deacons should have only one wife, thereby setting an example that would eventually clear a Christian community of multiple marriages. 1 Timothy 3:2, 12.

B. In the Old Testament a mate that was guilty of adultery was stoned to death, thereby making the marriage contract completely void! Leviticus 18:20, 29; 20:10; Deuteronomy 22:22-27; Proverbs 6:29. Divorce in Old Testament times did not mean that the innocent party was forbidden to have again a marriage partner! Unfaithfulness was as final as death, since the guilty part was killed. A person whose guilty mate was killed, was at complete liberty to marry again. Romans 7:2.

WE CONCLUDE, therefore, that the Old Testament Law contained an element of mercy — and an awareness of basic physical needs — that is generally overlooked by some Christians. Exodus 20:14; Deuteronomy 24:1-4; Leviticus 19:20-22.

12. WHEN A PERSON BECOMES A CHRISTIAN ARE THEY SUPPOSED TO LEAVE THEIR UNSAVED MATE?

Absolutely not! A normal marriage relationship should be maintained which, if anything, will convert the unsaved. 1 Corinthians 7:16; 1 Peter 3:1. Read 1 Corinthians 7:11-14: ". . . let him not put her away . . . let her not leave him . . . ."

13. CAN UNBELIEVERS, WHO HAVE BEEN DIVORCED AND REMARRIED BECOME CHRISTIANS AND RECEIVE RIGHT-STANDING WITH GOD?

Yes, if they repent of this sin of adultery. Unbelievers can be cleansed in the blood of Christ, justified and sanctified in the Name of our Lord Jesus Christ and by the Spirit of our God. God will forgive them and remove the stain of the past far from them that they might become citizens of the Kingdom of God.

When a person becomes a Christian, they should then begin living the Christian life in the situation in which they find themselves. A person, for instance, who has been married several times, with children from both marriages, cannot leave the present mate and try to reconcile with a former mate. Marital tangles are so involved these days that it is best and sanest for a person to start serving God in his present situation — trusting God for the forgiveness of the past and strength for the future. 1 Corinthians 6:9-11. Jesus said: "Go and sin no more." John 8:11.

14. WHAT IS THE HUSBAND'S POSITION IN THE HOME?

The husband is to exercise the government and leadership of the home. God says that "the husband is the head of the wife." Ephesians 5:22, 23. He is the protector, provider, priest, the strong, the noble. He should be the glory of his children and the joy of his wife. Proverbs 17:6; Ephesians 5:24, 25, 23 (read the Amplified Translation of this).

15. HOW SHOULD HUSBANDS REGARD THEIR WIVES?

"Husbands, love your wives . . . as Christ also loved . . . love their wives as their own bodies . . . every one of you in particular so love his wife even as himself . . . ." Ephesians 5:23-25.

16. WHAT IS THE WIFE'S POSITION IN THE HOME?

The wife is to be a help MEET for her husband. God has so constructed woman that she is a wonderful compliment to man. Faith, spiritual insight and a sympathetic, loving nature were created within her that she might be his source of encouragement and strength in times of difficulty and distress. Genesis 2:18.

17. HOW SHOULD WIVES REGARD THEIR HUSBANDS?

Wives should be in subjection to their husbands so that they might please God. A saved woman can actually win an unbelieving husband to Christ by her willful subjection and godly life. 1 Peter 3:1, 2 (Amplified).

18. WHAT IS THE GREAT SECRET OF A HAPPY HOME?

The great secret of a happy home is LOVE! Happy the home where God is and love fills every heart! Proverbs 15:17; Song of Solomon 8:6, 7.

LESSON 1 STUDY QUESTIONS BASED ON "MARRIAGE IS A SACRAMENT"

1. Define the meaning of "sacrament."
2. What is the Sacrament of Marriage?
3. What preparation does God require of those entering marriage?
4. What should engaged couples seek?

5. When are two people considered compatible in marriage?
6. What two basic marriage laws should not be violated?
7. How does God regard divorce?
8. What are the major reasons for divorce in our society?
9. Do the same reasons motivate Christians to separate?
10. Does God ever give permission to dissolve the marriage covenant?
11. What two important differences exist between the society of Bible times and the present?
12. When a person becomes a Christian are they supposed to leave their unsaved mate?
13. Can unbelievers, who have been divorced and remarried, become Christians and receive right-standing with God?
14. What is the husband's position in the home?
15. How should husbands regard their wives?
16. What is the wife's position in the home?
17. How should wives regard their husbands?
18. What is the great secret of a happy home?

LESSON 2: THE DEDICATION OF CHILDREN

1. WHAT IS THE SACRAMENT OF THE DEDICATION OF CHILDREN?

    This sacrament is the solemn presentation of a child to God. This is done when the parents (or guardians) of a child bring the child before the presbytery of the local church and make covenant between themselves and God. Hands are laid upon the child and parents, and the blessing of God invoked upon them. This is in obedience to Christ's command. Matthew 19:14; Mark 10:16.

2. WHAT COVENANT IS MADE BETWEEN GOD AND THE PARENTS IN THIS SACRAMENT?

    In the Sacrament of Marriage, a covenant is made between a man, a woman and God. When a child is born from this union, the child is also brought into the covenant of God's blessing through dedication by the parents. Thus the child is placed within the sanctifying covenant bounds made between GOD-MAN-WOMAN. God promises blessings of peace, health, understanding and protection to the child whose parents promise to rear him for the service of the Lord. 1 Samuel 1:27, 28; Psalms 127:3.

3. WHAT ATTITUDE SHOULD THE PARENTS HAVE IN THIS SACRAMENT?

    They must be willing to assume the responsibility of raising and training the child in the ways of God. It does not mean that the parents must dedicate their child to become a minister or missionary but rather that they want the child to fulfill his own destiny in God's purposes. The parents' job will be to raise the child in such a Christian atmosphere that the child will automatically desire to continue in such a way of life.

    The Prayer of the parents should be:

    "O my Lord . . . teach us what we shall do unto the child that shall be born" (or, "the child you have given us to rear for thee"). Judges 13:8, 12.

4. SHOULD INFANTS BE BAPTIZED?

    No. Only those who are old enough to understand the meaning of repentance and believing in the Lord Jesus Christ should be baptized. This an infant cannot do. Mark 16:16; Acts 2:38, 41.

5. HOW THEN CAN DEDICATED INFANTS, WHO HAVE NEVER BEEN BAPTIZED, ENTER INTO THE KINGDOM OF HEAVEN IF THEY DIE BEFORE THEY ARE OLD ENOUGH TO REPENT AND BE BAPTIZED?

    Children are sanctified (made holy) by the faith of their believing parents. Children, born into a Christian home and presented to God in dedication, are kept by the power of God. They are made holy by the faith of their parents until they reach "the age of accountability" (the time in life when they can properly decide for themselves); at that time they assume the responsibility for their own repentance and baptism.

"Otherwise, your children would be unclean, unblessed heathen, outside the Christian covenant. But as it is, they are prepared for God, pure and clean." 1 Corinthians 7:14, Amplified New Testament.

6.   IN WHAT STATE ARE INFANTS WHO ARE NOT DEDICATED TO GOD, THE CHILDREN OF UNBELIEVING PARENTS?
The children of unbelieving parents who have not been presented to God in dedication, are considered unclean, unblessed heathen. Again note 1 Corinthians 7:14; also, Joshua 7:1-26; Genesis 7:13. We see, therefore, a real ministry of evangelism for the Sunday School in the converting and training of the children of unsaved parents. It is our conviction that we must do all we can to win them, but leave the final judgment in God's hands; God's mercy and justice will do that which is right in the lives of undedicated babies and small children. Genesis 18:25.

7.   WHAT IS THE AGE OF ACCOUNTABILITY?
We believe that children are under the protection of the covenant made at the time of their dedication until they reach approximately 12 years of age. At that time, they should be thoroughly trained in doctrine and brought to a decision for Jesus Christ. They then must enter covenant with God by way of personal repentance, faith, the cleansing of the blood and circumcision of heart in water baptism. Note that Jesus became a "Son of the Law" (and accountable to God for his life) when he was 12 years of age. Luke 2:42.

8.   HOW DILIGENTLY SHOULD PARENTS TEACH CHILDREN GOD'S WORD?
"These words, which I command thee this day, shall be in thine heart: and thou shalt teach them diligently unto thy children, and shalt talk of them when thou sittest in thine house; and when thou walkest by the way, when thou liest down, and when thou risest up." Deuteronomy 6:6, 7.

9.   HOW SHOULD PARENTS TRAIN THEIR CHILDREN?
Some thoughts from Proverbs:

  3:11 — Chastening is a sign of real parental love!
13:24 — God says you hate your son if you spare the rod!
19:18 — Chasten while the child is young, and there is still hope!
22:6 — Properly trained, the child in later life won't depart from God.
22:15 — The rod drives out foolishness; it breaks the stubborn will!
23:13 — Beat with the rod, he will not die (just be uncomfortable)!
23:14 — The rod (in proper discipline) will deliver your child from hell.
29:15 — The rod and reproof brings wisdom; childish self-will, shame!
29:17 — Rest and delight will come when children are disciplined!

10. AGAINST WHAT EVIL SHOULD FATHERS GUARD?

"Fathers, provoke not your children to anger, lest they be discouraged." Colossians 3:21. The Scriptures listed under No. 9 should not be interpreted to mean physical abuse. Also, carnal anger — especially when there is no justifiable reason — will only frustrate the child. Firm, consistent discipline will direct the will of the child, bringing him into proper subjection, and yet allow him to develop a sense of duty and what is right. Time spent in explanation, prayer, proper fun, etc., will counterbalance the rod of discipline and produce wholesome young people.

11. WHEN DOES THE PARENT'S RESPONSIBILITY TO GOD FOR THEIR CHILDREN END?

A parent's responsibility to God for his children never ends. He must be ever faithful to pray for them, admonish them and encourage them to serve God. When a child is confirmed in the faith as it is in Jesus Christ, he renews the covenant his parents made with God at the time of his dedication. This transfers the responsibility of his soul's salvation to the child himself.

12. WHAT QUESTION MUST EVERY UNFAITHFUL PARENT MEET?

"Where is the flock that was given thee, thy beautiful flock?" Jeremiah 13:20. Happy will those parents be who can say, "Behold, here am I and the children the Lord hath given me." Isaiah 8:18.

LESSON 2 STUDY QUESTIONS BASED ON
"THE SACRAMENT OF THE DEDICATION OF CHILDREN"

1. What is the Sacrament of the Dedication of Children?
2. What covenant is made between God and the parents in this sacrament?
3. What attitude should the parents have in this sacrament?
4. Should infants be baptized?
5. How then can dedicated infants, who have never been baptized, enter into the Kingdom of Heaven if they die before they are old enough to repent and be baptized?
6. In what state are infants who are not dedicated to God, the children of unbelieving parents?
7. What is the age of accountability?
8. How diligently should parents teach children God's Word?
9. How should parents discipline their children?
10. Against what evil should fathers guard?
11. When does the parent's responsibility to God for their children end?
12. What question must every unfaithful parent meet?

LESSON 3: GOD LOVES A CHEERFUL GIVER!

1. ARE WE EXPECTED TO GIVE OUR SUBSTANCE TO GOD?

   We cannot escape the frequency of Bible references on giving, and it becomes obvious that a vital part of fellowship with God is the worshipful act of offering our substance to Him. This principle is one which remains unchanged in both Old and New Testaments. Genesis 4:4; Mark 12:41-44.

2. WHAT DOES IT MEAN TO TITHE?

   To tithe is to give or pay a tenth part of our income or substance for the support of God's program.

3. WHERE IS THE TITHE TO BE GIVEN?

   In the Old Testament time, the tithes and offerings were brought to the "storehouse" (Malachi 3:10; Nehemiah 13:12) which meant the local place designated by the spiritual leadership for the storage and disbursement of the people's substance. In the New Testament the same principle applies to the church's operation, with the people of a given area bringing their support to recognized local leadership (Acts 4:34, 35; 1 Corinthians 16:1-3, 2 Corinthians 8 and 9). This indicates that your tithe should be given in the support of that local church program that ministers to your spiritual needs.

4. WHERE DOES TITHING FIRST APPEAR IN THE BIBLE?

   A. ABRAHAM (Genesis 14), 430 years BEFORE the Law, gave God tithes! He tithed as a result of a revelation of one of God's names (v. 20), not by a compulsion of the Law. Abraham spurned the spoil of the grateful kings, for he had met the God who possessed all things.

   B. JACOB (Genesis 28), was aware of the amount due to God, but was reluctant to give it. A revelation of God's presence gave him a desire to give and enter covenant.

   THEREFORE, we have two classic examples of tithing in the first book of the Bible: wealthy Abraham and penniless (at this time) Jacob.

5. WHAT TYPE OF GIVING WAS DEMANDED UNDER THE LAW OF MOSES?
   Three tithes are mentioned, and also strong admonitions about being liberal to the poor and strangers.

   A. "THE LORD'S TITHE" or "THE LEVITICAL TITHE" was for the support of the priesthood. Leviticus 27:30-33; Numbers 18:21-32. The tithe included one tenth of all possessions, nothing was exempt. The ministry was just as obligated to tithe as the people.

   B. THE SECOND TITHE or "THE FESTIVAL TITHE" was for worship, joy and maintaining the fear of God. Deuteronomy 14:22-27. Those who find it difficult to give find it difficult to worship. This tithe

185

consisted of the yearly increase and was eaten and enjoyed by the tither himself at the God-ordained meeting place.

C. THE THIRD TITHE for the poor came every three years, and insured the blessing of God upon the donors. Deuteronomy 14:28, 29. This was given to the widows, the fatherless, the strangers and Levites.

D. ADDITIONAL GIVING. There was to be a further giving of substance to the poor and strangers. Leviticus 19:9, 10; Deuteronomy 24:19-21. Note Ruth 2:2-17. And, as if that is not enough, note the ultimate tithe: giving one out of every ten people for God's service! Nehemiah 11:1, 2.

6. DURING REVIVAL PERIODS, TITHING WAS ALWAYS RE-ESTABLISHED.
Spiritual people desire to give, but cold hearts have no interest in tithing. 2 Chronicles 31:5-12; Nehemiah 10:37; 38; 12:44; 13:5, 22.

7. DID THE OLD TESTAMENT PROPHETS EVER MENTION TITHING?
Absolutely! Malachi links God's unchanging nature with tithing (3:6-12). Haggai the prophet thundered "Consider your ways!" (1:5). When God's people dwelt in tents, God was content to dwell in a tent also. When they prospered and began to live in houses, God also chose to dwell in a house. Compare Deuteronomy 28 with Haggai 1 – God has a way of relieving us of our money (often with interest) to show us our failure. Note: Ecclesiastes 7:12; Proverbs 11:24, 25; 3:9, 10; Psalms 10:3.

8. WHAT WAS JESUS' ATTITUDE ABOUT GIVING?
In Matthew 23:23 Jesus commended the Pharisees' tithing, but condemned their ommissions. Jesus' teaching about "alms" refers to the "Third Tithe" mentioned in Question 5. The Lord's Tithe goes to the ministry and church, while alms go to poor individuals. Matthew 6: 4. Jesus watched people giving, Luke 21:1-4. Matthew 6:19 links the heart with the treasure.

We should be liberal: Matthew 10:8; Luke 6:38; Acts 20:35.
Riches are deceitful: Matthew 13:22; Luke 12:15-34.
Perfection conquers the love of money: Matthew 19:16-30.
Jesus' own ministry was supported by others: Luke 8:1-3.

9. TRACE THE TRAGIC ROUTE OF JUDAS' LIFE:
Matthew 10:5-8, 9-14; John 12:6; 6:71; 13:2; Luke 22:3; Matthew 26:14; Mark 14:10; Acts 1:25.

"For the love of money is the root of all evil: which while some coveted after, they have erred from the faith, and pierced themselves through with many sorrows." 1 Timothy 6:10.

10. IS IT RIGHT FOR CHRISTIANS TO TITHE THEIR MONEY FOR THE SUP-
PORT OF THEIR SPIRITUAL LEADERS? SHOULDN'T PASTORS WORK?
Paul clearly teaches in 1 Corinthians 9:1-14 that just as the Levitical priesthood lived from the people's tithes, so also should the New Testament
ministry. "Even so HATH THE LORD ORDAINED that they which preach
the Gospel should live of the Gospel" (9:14). Soldiers, farmers, etc., are
rightly paid their wages, so it must be with the ministry — "The labourer
is worthy of his reward." 1 Timothy 5:17, 18. Note that Paul quotes the
Law which allows the ox to eat while it grinds.

Although Paul did not allow the Corinthian Church to support him (for
circumstantial reasons), he says, "forgive me this wrong." 2 Corinthians
12:13. Jesus was supported by others (Luke 8:1-3), and he taught his
disciples to rely on others (Luke 10:3-11). Early in the disciples' training
they were taught that from now on they were to catch men, or be fishers of
men. To supply the natural needs of his ministry, Jesus told Peter to go and
catch a fish, and the fish would have the needed money (Matthew 17:27).
Jesus is still meeting the needs of the ministry by this method: the ones
who are ministered to in spiritual things are required to minister natural
things in return. The Gospel is to be given freely to the heathen, but when
the heathen are converted, God expects them to supply the needs of the
ministry. Galatians 6:6; 1 Timothy 6:18.

11. DIDN'T PAUL THE APOSTLE DO SECULAR WORK FOR A LIVING?
When he did, it was the exception rather than the rule. Most of his ministry
to the churches was on a "full-time" basis. When he did work, it was to set
an example or to help get a church started. Paul worked with his hands at
Corinth (Acts 18:3), but also received offerings from other churches to
maintain himself while he was there (1 Corinthians 9:15, 2 Corinthians
11:7-9; 12:13; Philippians 4:13), and he didn't plan to receive anything for
himself on his third visit (2 Corinthians 12:14). It also appears that he did
some secular work at Thessalonica (1 Thessalonians 2:6, 9; 2 Thessalonians
3:8), but also received some offerings from Philippi to help support himself
while he was there. It also seems that Paul did some work with his hands
at Ephesus (Acts 20:34, 35). We find, therefore, ONE specific reference to
his tent making, with the possibility of his having worked in secular work in
THREE of the many cities where he preached. 2 Thessalonians 3:6-15 gives
the reason for what secular work he did do — to set an example of diligence
before the converted heathen who tended toward laziness.

12. OFFERINGS "FOR THE SAINTS" IN THE NEW TESTAMENT CHURCHES.
1 Corinthians 16:1-3 was an order. The giving was to be weekly, and that
upon the Lord's Day or the first day of the week. "Every one of you"

was to participate. It was to be based on the only fair system — in proportion to how much God had prospered them. Romans 12:13; 15:25-28; Acts 24:17; 11:29; 1 Timothy 5:10, 15; Galatians 2:10.

KEY CHAPTERS are 2 Corinthians 8 and 9. Prove your love by your giving! God's love is assured to the cheerful giver (9:7). The principle of sowing and reaping is explained. IT IS SIGNIFICANT that the TWO thoughts of worship and joy that are associated with the Old Testament tithe are emphasized (9:7 and 11 to 13).

13. WHAT SHOULD OUR ATTITUDE TOWARD MONEY BE?

Our prosperity should not cause us to be lukewarm, but rather, we should prosper materially as we prosper spiritually — so that we can handle the increase in a godly way! 3 John 2. But gain is not godliness! 1 Timothy 6:9 and 10 give us a key thought and a tremendous warning. Every person seeking to be delivered from evil should certainly be cutting off this root first!

14. DOES THE NEW TESTAMENT TEACH TITHING?

Tithing is mentioned in seven verses of the New Testament. The first two occurences give the striking statement of Jesus Himself:

"Yes, you should tithe, but you shouldn't leave the more important things undone." Matthew 23:23; Luke 11:42 (Living Gospels Translation).

In addition to Jesus' statement, we also have the apostolic teaching in Hebrews 7:5-10. Here we find that the "Order of Melchisedec" involves giving tithes to God Himself in spontaneous worship, rather than as a legal obligation to a dying order of earthly priests. Hebrews 7 shows that tithing under the Law was merely the legal, outward manifestation of a higher principle — the faith that sprung joyfully from the heart of "Father Abraham" as he gave tithe to the eternal priesthood of the living Lord Jesus! This is how we should give today, not grudgingly, but with genuine joy and worship (2 Corinthians 9:7).

LESSON 3 STUDY QUESTIONS BASED ON
"GOD LOVES A CHEERFUL GIVER!"

1. Are we expected to give our substance to God?
2. What does it mean to tithe?
3. Where is the tithe to be given?
4. Where does tithing first appear in the Bible?
5. What type of giving was demanded under the Law of Moses?

LESSON 3 STUDY QUESTIONS BASED ON
"GOD LOVES A CHEERFUL GIVER!" (Continued)

6. What effect did revival have on tithing?
7. Did the Old Testament prophets ever mention tithing?
8. What was Jesus attitude about giving?
9. What was the basic problem in the life of Judas?
10. Is it right for Christians to tithe their money for the support of pastors?
11. Didn't Paul the apostle do secular work for a living?
12. What was said about "offerings for the saints" in the New Testament?
13. What should our attitude toward money be?
14. Does the New Testament teach tithing?

LESSON 4: THE IMPORTANCE OF FASTING

1. WHAT IS FASTING?

    The Bible does not define "fasting," but it is a word with a universally accepted meaning. Random House Dictionary says: "1. to abstain from all food. 2. to eat only sparingly or of certain kinds of food, esp. as a religious observance." Webster adds: "religious mortification by abstinence." (Note Colossians 3:5).

2. DOES FASTING MEAN THAT YOU DON'T DRINK WATER, COFFEE, ETC?

    Fasting means to do without food entirely, but does not exclude the use of pure water. Water is in no way stimulating to the bodily appetites. On any fast which continues for more than a few days, the drinking of water is essential. Moses was so supernaturally aided that he neither ate food or drank water for 40 days, but this was the exception rather than the rule. If you take coffee, etc. etc., you are not really fasting in the primary sense of the word, but if you do it as unto the Lord, it could be termed a "partial fast." The Bible does not go into the definition of fasting.

3. DOES FASTING INJURE THE HUMAN BODY OR MIND?

    Proper fasting does not injure the body or mind. If anything, it will bring you better physical health and enable your mental faculties to function more clearly. For the first few days of a fast, a person will feel quite weak; then, after a few days of fasting, strength will begin to return even as the fast continues.

    Fasting is not starvation! Sometimes we confuse hunger and appetite. For instance, a person who has a craving for food that is based on habit has an appetite. When a few meals are missed, stomach "pains" are the demand of appetite for satisfaction. True hunger doesn't begin until the end of a long fast, and this may take weeks (perhaps up to 40 days). Actual body hunger begins when all waste tissue is used up by the body.

    Some people get a headache after one day of fasting. Often this can be traced to the person's improper eating habits, excessive coffee drinking, eating of sweets, etc. It is also possible for a person to have a basic physical ailment that would affect the way in which he feels during the fast; such a condition necessitates great care in determining the intensity and duration of the fast.

    Do not be alarmed by headaches, slight fever and bad breath. The oxidising of waste materials by the body systems is responsible for these reactions. This is why it is ESSENTIAL to drink a lot of water, preferably six glasses a day; this helps the natural elimination handle the waste material more efficiently. There is actually a very real physical profit in fasting. The body undergoes a period of rest and cleansing that is of great value. At the same time, the mind, emotions and spirit of the person undergo a remarkable

sharpening of perception and a deepened sensitivity to the more important things in life. A new devotion to God takes place, a true humility
becomes evident, and a new deeper appreciation for simple necessities
takes over.

4. **SHOULD A PERSON WHO IS ON MEDICATION STOP TAKING IT DURING A FAST?**

It is best for the individual to determine this for himself. If he is taking
heavy medication, it would be best to have his physician's opinion.

5. **THERE IS MORE TO FASTING THAN JUST ABSTAINING FROM FOOD!**

Fasting is not some kind of an endurance contest. It is not a form of
penance. Some feel that the more they fast the more power they will have
to force God to do what they want of Him. The mere act of abstaining
from food does not move the hand of God. We are not to be like a group
of prisoners on a hunger strike who are determined to change the attitude
of the warden.

As a person fasts, he should endeavor to spend as much time in prayer as
possible. If he is working, he should take the coffee breaks and lunch period
for prayer. Often people feel that since they cannot eat that they should
just go to bed. It does not hurt a person to fast for a day or two and work
at the same time. If the mental attitude is right, a person will actually
benefit from the experience. It is important to maintain physical exercise.
On long fasts it is best not to work, but to retire somewhere for much
prayer and Bible reading.

Great results will come from periods of praying in the Spirit during a fast.
During the time the fast is being broken, a fresh quickening will come to
the body. The tendency will be to use up this new strength in eating, but
if the person will hold his appetite to reasonable amounts of food and pray
a great deal, God will answer prayer in a wonderful way.

6. **DID ANY OF THE GREAT PEOPLE OF THE BIBLE CONSIDER FASTING IMPORTANT?**

Moses: Exodus 32:28; Deuteronomy 9:9, 18.
David: Psalms 35:13; 69:10; 109:24; 2 Samuel 12:16-23.
Nehemiah: Nehemiah 1:4.
Daniel: Daniel 6:18, 9:3.
Elijah: 1 Kings 19:8.
Jesus: Matthew 4:2.
Paul: 2 Corinthians 6:5; 11:27.
Cornelius: Acts 10:30.
Anna: Luke 2:37.

Ahab: 1 Kings 21:27 (even this wicked king found favor with God through fasting).

7. ON OCCASION, WHOLE GROUPS PARTICIPATED IN JOINT FASTING.
Israel before Sinai: Exodus 19:10, 11.
Israel before Jordan and Circumcision: Joshua 3:4.
Jehoshaphat called a fast: 2 Chronicles 20:3.
During time of restoration: Ezra 8:21, 23; Nehemiah 9:1.
Nineveh's repentance: Jonah 3:5.
Note these references: Judges 20:26; 1 Samuel 7:6; 31:13; 2 Samuel 1:12;
1 Chronicles 10:12; Esther 4:3, 16; 9:31; Jeremiah 36:6, 9; Joel 1:14;
2:12, 15.

8. WAS FASTING ONLY FOR OLD TESTAMENT TIMES?
It is a timeless principle. If anything, it has been amplified and given new significance since the Cross. Isaiah 58:3-6.

9. FASTING IS TAUGHT IN THE NEW TESTAMENT AS A PART OF THE NEW COVENANT.

A. JESUS' TEACHING:
Matthew 6:16   – One of the key thoughts in the Sermon on the Mt.
Matthew 17:21   – Overcoming Satan by fasting and prayer.
Matthew 9:15   – His answer to John's disciples.
Mark 2:18-20; Luke 5:33-35 – His answer to scribes and Pharisees.

B. THE EARLY CHURCH PRACTICED FASTING:
Acts 9:9   – Saul began his Christian life fasting.
Acts 12:5   – The Early Church prayed WITHOUT CEASING (no coffee or lunch breaks!).
Acts 13:2   – The Church at Antioch fasted, then sent Paul forth.
Acts 14:23   – They prayed with fasting as they ordained elders.
Acts 27:9, 21, 33 – Paul and others on 14 day fast.

C. IN THE EPISTLES:
1 Corinthians 7:5   – Advice to married couples about fasting.
2 Corinthians 6:5   – Fasting is one way ministers approve themselves.
2 Corinthians 11:17 – Paul fasted often.
1 Timothy 5:5   – An unusual ministry for desolate widows.

10. DOES A CHRISTIAN DISPLEASE GOD IF HE DOESN'T FAST?
Many Christians have never fasted a day in their lives, and many evangelical churches even teach that it is not necessary for our day. You, of course, must make up your own mind on the subject, but every Christian should seriously consider the implications of Jesus' teaching on three different occasions:

A. IN THE SERMON ON THE MOUNT, Jesus stated very simply: "Moreover when ye fast . . . but thou, when thou fastest . . . ." Matthew 6:16, 17. It appears that Jesus assumes that His followers will fast!

B. JESUS TOLD JOHN'S FOLLOWERS: ". . . then shall they fast." Matthew 9:16. He made it clear that while He was with his disciples they did not need to fast, but when he would leave them, then they would!

C. JESUS TOLD THE SCRIBES AND PHARISEES: ". . . and then shall they fast in those days." Luke 5:35.

11. HOW DO YOU CONDUCT YOURSELF DURING A FAST?

Jesus clearly teaches us in Matthew 6:17 that we are not to conduct ourselves so that others are aware of our fasting. Wash yourself, comb your hair, dress normally. We are not to make a spectacle out of ourselves.

12. HOW OFTEN SHOULD WE FAST?

The Pharisees made a practice of fasting twice a week. Luke 18:12; 5:33; Matthew 9:14. The Church Fathers felt that the early church fasted twice a week, on Wednesday and Friday. John Wesley felt this strongly, and no Methodist preacher could hold his ordination in early days unless he fasted twice a week. You must decide this for yourself, since the Bible does not specify the time. Once a week would not hurt anyone, and certainly every church should call several days of fasting and prayer once every few months.

13. HOW SHOULD A PERSON BREAK A FAST?

Take as long to break a fast as you took to fast. Break the fast with fruit juices (not milk). Then go to soups and light food. Do not gorge on hamburgers, etc., after several days of fasting, or you will make yourself sick. As you break the fast, you will then feel the real power of the fast. Restrain yourself from heavy eating and pray as much as possible.

LESSON 4 STUDY QUESTIONS BASED ON
"THE IMPORTANCE OF FASTING"

1. What is fasting?
2. Does fasting mean that you do not drink water, coffee, etc.?
3. Does fasting injure the human body or mind?
4. Should a person who is on medication stop taking it during a fast?
5. Is there more to fasting than just abstaining from food?
6. Did any of the great people of the Bible consider fasting important?
7. Name some of the occasions when whole groups participated in joint fasting.

8. Was fasting only for Old Testament times?
9. Is fasting taught in the New Testament as a part of the new covenant? Where?
10. Does a Christian displease God if he does not fast?
11. How do you conduct yourself during a fast?
12. How often should we fast?
13. How should a person break a fast?

LESSON 5: THIS IS YOUR LIFE

INTRODUCTION:

This last lesson of the catechism course is to help you orient yourself to the basic areas of practical Christian experience. All of the previous Bible knowledge is valueless unless you can live victoriously and effectively in your personal life.

YOUR LIFE IS LIKE A WHEEL:

Your life is like a wheel with five spokes. Christ is the hub of the wheel — the center of strength. The outer wheel is your life, and the five spokes represent the five major relationships of your life. For a "well-rounded" experience through Christ, it is vitally important that each of the five spokes are strong and true.

THE FIVE SPOKES REPRESENT YOUR RELATIONSHIP TO:

[1]   God
[2]   Self
[3]   Family
[4]   Church
[5]   World

In our previous lessons, the answers are provided for you. Now, however, we present questions which only you can answer. To direct your thinking we have provided a few categories for you to consider under each of the relationships.

1.   HOW IS MY RELATIONSHIP TO GOD?
[1]   As a Son? Galatians 4:5-7.
[2]   As a Priest? 1 Peter 2:9.
[3]   As a Steward? Matthew 25:31-46.
[4]   As a Friend? John 15:15.

2.   HOW IS MY RELATIONSHIP TO SELF?
[1]   Am I a daily Bible reader? 2 Timothy 2:15.
[2]   Is worship and prayer a part of my daily life? Hebrews 13:15.
[3]   Am I an active part of my home church? 1 Corinthians 12.

3.   HOW IS MY RELATIONSHIP TO MY FAMILY?
[1]   Do I cooperate with the other members? Ephesians 5:2.
[2]   Am I an obedient child? Ephesians 6:4.
[3]   Am I an understanding parent? Ephesians 6:1-3.
[4]   Do I truly love my marriage partner? Ephesians 5:22, 25.

4.   HOW IS MY RELATIONSHIP TO THE CHURCH?
[1]   Am I planted where God wants me? Psalms 92:13.

[2] Am I a functioning member of Christ's Body? Romans 12.

[3] Am I assuming my full responsibilities? Galatians 6:2.

[4] Do I discern the Body of Christ? 1 Corinthians 11:29.

5. HOW IS MY RELATIONSHIP TO THE WORLD?

[1] As an example of the believers? 1 Timothy 4:12.

[2] As a faithful witness of Jesus Christ? Acts 1:8.

[3] As an effective soul winner? Proverbs 11:30.

[4] Am I above reproach with my fellow workmen? Ephesians 6:5-9.

LESSON 5 STUDY QUESTIONS BASED ON "THIS IS YOUR LIFE"

1. How is my relationship to God?
2. How is my relationship to self?
3. How is my relationship to my family?
4. How is my relationship to the Church?
5. How is my relationship to the World?

THE END

INDEX

197

INDEX